Are We Autistic Towards God

(A Scientist's Probe into
How We can Get Connected with God)

Books Published by Allied Publishers for Dr. Siddhartha Ganguli

1. Live Happily, Work Happily - 2009
3rd Reprint 2014
2. SUCCESS Can be Planned and Earned - 2010
1st Reprint 2013
3. Greying Gracefully: Planning for Retirement and Old Age Happiness - 2011
4. Conscious Management - 2011
5. The Making of a Winning Child - 2012
6. Smart Leading and Parenting of Teenage Kids in the Digital Era - 2021
7. Music is Magic Music is Medicine: Impact of Music on Body, Brain, Mind & Soul - 2023
8. The Four Moons in the Human Body The Mysterious Tales of the Bauls of Bengal (Introducing 'BaulOlogy') - 2023
9. Love: A Good MedicineThe Saga of the Elixir of Life (Introducing 'LoveOlogy') - 2024
10. Goddess Kali God Thoughts Sri Sri Ramakrishna and A Few Slices of Sri Sri Ramakrishna's Soul (Introducing 'SoulOlogy') - 2024
11. The 'Real' Ramakrishna: As I Have Come to Know Him as Ramakrishna's Child - 2024
12. The Third Eye: The Mystery of Sri Sri Ramakrishna's Visions - 2024
13. The Five-Faced Hindu God - 2025

Are We Autistic Towards God

(A Scientist's Probe into
How We can Get Connected with God)

Siddhartha Ganguli, ***PhD***

Winner of
Golden Book Prize – 2025
International Authorship Excellence Award – 2025
&
Golden Wings Book Prize – 2026

ALLIED PUBLISHERS PVT. LTD.

Noida • Mumbai • Kolkata • Chennai

ALLIED PUBLISHERS PRIVATE LIMITED

D-5, Sector-2, **Noida**–201 301
Ph. Nos.: 0120-4320295/2542557/4352866
E-mail: delhi.books@alliedpublishers.com

17 Chittaranjan Avenue, **Kolkata**–700072
Ph.: 033-22129618 • E-mail: cal.books@alliedpublishers.com

15 J.N. Heredia Marg, Ballard Estate, **Mumbai**–400001
Ph.: 022-42126969 • E-mail: mumbai.books@alliedpublishers.com

No. 25/10, Commander-in-Chief Road, Ethiraj Lane (Next to Post Office)
Egmore, **Chennai**–600008
Ph.: 044-28223938 • E-mail: chennai.books@alliedpublishers.com

Website: https://alliedpublishers.in

ISBN: 978-93-48699-56-5

The theme of the front cover has been designed by the author's young creative friend Andy J. Peters from Manchester, England, U.K.

Published by Sunil Sachdev and printed by Ravi Sachdev
at Allied Publishers Pvt. Ltd., D-5, Sector-2, Noida–201 301

Dedication

This very special volume is dedicated to the immortal souls of all prophets, avatars and God incarnates as they had all physically existed on this planet

Acknowledgements

I acknowledge, with heart-felt love and respect, the active cooperation of Allied Publishers Pvt. Ltd., Noida, UP, India for undertaking the entire responsibility of publication, promotion and distribution of this very special literary work of mine.

The constant encouragement of my wife Utpala and my three children Abhishek-Abhirup-Ishita has been most motivating as much as the good wishes of my readers from all over the world.

The unstinted vigil of my Personal Secretary Pervez Alam has been most helpful all through this book project.

I must make special mention of the reputed American neuro-surgeon Michael Egnor. MD and Professor Jeffrey Kripal, PhD of Rice University, Texas, USA who allowed me to use their lives' extraordinary mystical experiences as case studies.

I am so happy that Professor Norbert Ammerman, PhD of the University of Osnabruck, Germany, who is a world authority on Religious Studies, readily agreed to write the Foreword of this unusual treatise.

I am grateful to my young creative friend Andy J. Peters from Manchester, England, U.K. for creating the theme of the front cover of this book.

Contents

Foreword

There are authors whose books you read – and there are authors whose books read you. For me, Dr. Siddhartha Ganguli is one of those rare people whose work not only imparts knowledge, but also opens up spaces: spaces in which the spiritual, the physical and the divine no longer have to contradict each other.

Anyone who picks up this book should be prepared for the fact that the familiar categories are not enough. Ganguli is not an academic theologian, a neuropsychologist in the strict sense, a mystic in the traditional sense – and it is precisely because of this that he succeeds in something that would hardly be possible in the classical disciplines: **he combines the innermost movements of the human being with the great movements of the divine and takes our brain seriously without losing the secret.**

A view that is new – and that allows us to see ourselves in a new way

Ganguli's thinking begins where others end: with the question of how the divine can appear in a biological being at all. His thesis that microorganisms, neuronal circuits, hormones and brain waves are not only biological phenomena, but **resonance chambers** in which the sacred reassures itself is as bold as it is inspiring.

What particularly impresses me about him is the refusal to reduce human experience to mere neurobiology. For him, trauma is not only a deficit, but a threshold; not just a wound, but an opening. He shows – on the basis of case histories, mythical lines, personal experience – how borderline moments of life are at the same time borderline moments of consciousness, in which reality rearranges itself and God shines through for a moment.

Man as God's organ of perception

Ganguli reverses a classical perspective: We not only strive to recognize God – **but God knows Himself through our neural architecture.** For him, the brain is not a closed apparatus, but a resonator, an instrument tuned for transcendence. This view is original, provocative and opens up ways of thinking that are rarely trodden in academic theology. He says himself that he "does not want to be academically alien to life in the best sense of the word". That he is not is due to a biography that has led from strictly empirical research in biomechanics to a metaphysical question about consciousness, gods, voices and sacred presence. It is a path that shows courage: from the measurable to the unspeakable.

A book that does not want to prove, but to transform

This work is something rare: **an attempt to bridge the fragmentation of our time in a salutary** way. Between science and mysticism, between neuropsychology and mythology, between trauma and revelation, between God and the brain.

Anyone who reads it senses that Ganguli does not explain anything from the outside, but from the inside. He doesn't think *about* the Divine – he thinks *from* the Divine.

Music, gods and gratitude – a personal touch

Our connection is not only that of science, but one of Resonanz.Er has listened to my music, picked it up, carried it on – and thus done something that goes beyond mere appreciation: he has embedded it in his own cosmos. And I discovered ways of thinking in his texts that I wouldn't have found on my own. Our conversations about Shaivism, consciousness, the presence of the divine in sound, the role of silence and the ways in which people experience God – they are among the most precious spiritual encounters of my life for me.

I owe him a lot: not only insights, but encouragement; not just thoughts, but connectedness.

So I don't read this book as a distanced scientist, but as someone who finds a musical, spiritual and human echo in Ganguli's thinking.

This book is an offer of dialogue: to science, to religion, to the soul of modern Menschen.Es challenges, it inspires, it opens. And it shows – in a time of distraction – that knowledge is possible if we have the courage to no longer think of body, mind and God separately.

Prof. Dr. Norbert AmmermannOsnabrück – Tiruvannamalai, 2025

Prof. Dr, Norbert Ammermann ev. Theologe kirchl . University Wuppertal Germany

"As a theologian, cultural scholar, and composer, he unites analytical clarity with a poetic musical language. His work explores the thresholds between religion, embodiment, perception, and sound, offering new pathways into contemporary spiritual experience."

htpps://norbert-ammermann.de

Rumi's Ruminations

"Come, come, wherever you are.
Wanderer, worshipper, lover of leaving.
It doesn't matter.
Ours is not a caravan of despair.
Come, even if you have broken your vows a thousand times.
Come yet again, come, come."

—**Jalaluddin Rumi** (1207–1273)
Sufi mystic

Where is God?

I tried to find Him on the Christian cross, but He was not there; I went to the Temples of the Hindus and to the old pagoda, but I could not find a trace of Him anywhere.

I searched the mountains and the valleys, but neither in the heights nor in the depths was I able to find Him. I went to the *Kaaba* in Mecca, but He was not there either.

I questioned the scholars and philosophers, but He was beyond their understanding. I then looked into my heart and it was there where He dwelled that I saw Him; He was nowhere else to be found.

—**Jalaluddin Rumi** (1207–1273)
Sufi Mystic

CHAPTER 1

Autistic God

God Had Been Autistic to the English Writer Somerset Maugham

God had been autistic to the English writer Somerset Maugham. He had lost faith in God from a very young age as God in whom he had been taught to believe had never responded to his prayers for relief from his purely personal problems. So, young Maugham had turned into an atheist and a lifelong non-believer. He simply could not put up with an autistic God.

Thus, although he lived the life of a most successful writer, travelling first class and residing in a spectacular villa on the French Riviera, Somerset Maugham (1874–1965) was restless. He was restless for that most elusive gift of all – spiritual enlightenment. Nevertheless, despite being an atheist, he wrote *The Making of a Saint*, the 1898 historical fiction novel regarding the spiritual and moral transformation of Filippo Brandolini in Renaissance Italy, or the more general process by which someone became recognized as a saint in the Catholic Church, which involves investigations into heroic virtue, beatification, and canonization, often requiring proof of miracles. This, to my mind, is the evidence of how curious Maugham was about what was the process of spiritual enlightenment even without the direct help of the entity called God.

With an introductory letter from an eminent friend and neighbour, the Aga Khan, he set off to India, where at a cocktail party in Chennai he was informed of a modern-day saint called the Maharshi who was living in Tiruvannamalai at the foot of the holy mountain, Arunachala.

In January 1938, Maugham set out on a journey to the Maharshi's ashram and reached there after a dull hot drive along a dusty, bumpy road. He and his companions were told that the Maharshi will see them in a little while. In the meantime, they sat down to eat up their picnic luncheon, but suddenly Maugham collapsed and fainted. From the car park, he was carried into a hut and laid on a bed made by wooden planks. When he regained his consciousness, he felt too weak to get up and move. The Maharshi was told what had happened and learning that the foreign guest was not well enough to come into the big hall in which the Saint ordinarily sat, he came out to the hut where Maugham was resting followed by two or three of his close devotees.

The Maharshi was bare-bodied; he was wearing only a loin cloth. But he was looking very neat, clean and almost dapper. One could feel his *aura*. He had a slight limp, walked slowly leaning on a stick. He didn't give the impression of a scholar but rather of a sweet-natured elderly peasant. He greeted, most cordially, the foreign guests who had brought for him a basket of fruits. He sat on the ground near the pallet on which Maugham was resting. The Saint gazed at Maugham's face and then, ceasing to look at him directly, he looked over his shoulder. Now and then, he tapped one of his feet on the earthen floor. The disciples present told Maugham later that he was concentrating in meditation upon him. Then, the Saint's gaze came back to Maugham and he asked if he wished to say anything to him or ask any question. Maugham was feeling weak and ill. He remained silent. The Maharshi said: "Silence is also conversation". He turned his head away and continued to look over Maugham's shoulder. Not a word was uttered by anyone present in the room. After another quarter of an hour, he got up, bowed, smiled and bade farewell. He stepped out of the hut quietly followed by his disciples.

What did Maugham gain from the *darshan*? The Saint was certainly not autistic as he exchanged positive eye contact, welcoming smile and cordial greetings. These loving gestures got him 'peace' and made him relaxed which were missing from his life. That was the hallmark of Ramana Maharshi's personality although he spoke very little and preferred to remain silent. Any mentally restless person who visited him would return with a calm and tranquil mind – *Beta*-negative brain wave (25 to 32 Hz) would turn into *Beta*-positive (14 to 25 Hz) and, if one had stayed longer in his company, would earn *alpha* brain wave (7 to 14 Hz) which is the source of creative insights.

When Maugham felt much better after a while, he got up and went to the hall where the Saint sat by the day and slept at night. The Swami, looked over Maugham's shoulder for a few minutes and then entered into the blissful state of meditation on the infinite, which is nothing else but *samadhi* leading to *delta* brain wave (0+ to 4 Hz).

The news of Maugham's fainting in the *ashram* was carried throughout India. Spiritual believers said that the Maharshi's *aura* had worked on him even before he met him in person. The Saint would have visited him in his *subtle body*. Many people came to see Maugham as the man who by the special grace of the Godman was rapt in the infinite. They believed that his soul had united with infinite reality which is *Brahma*. That experience did not convert Maugham who was an atheist but he came to believe in the spiritual vibrations of the saints. He detailed out his encounter with the Maharshi in his essay *The Saint*. And, it also served as the inspiration for the spiritual guru in his novel *The Razor's Edge*. He had plans to write one last book about *Adi Shankara*, the Hindu philosopher who consolidated the doctrine of *Advaita Vedanta* and spend his final days confined to a communal monastery. However, that dream of his never came true.

References

1. "W. Somerset Maugham: The Saint", *The Culturium*, 5th February 2017.
2. David Godman, "Somerset Maugham and The Razor's Edge", *The Mountain Path*, 1988, pp. 239–45.
3. "Ramana Ashram" – *Wikipedia*.

CHAPTER 2

Hearing Divine Voice

An Autistic Child Hears Virgin Mary's Voice

Tommy was a five-year-old boy in the State of Michigan in USA. His parents had died in a car crash soon after his birth and he was being raised by his grandmother, Susan. The child was autistic. He never spoke although he was very sober and sweet-natured. He used to play with his building blocks and other toys and a teddy bear which he had received as his first birthday gift was his constant companion. He used to get slightly irritated if there was any change in his meal times and if ever his grandma had served him food in crockeries which were different from his regular ones.

Tommy used to go for his regular speech therapy and physio-therapy sessions and would have his check-ups with his neurological consultant periodically. Two other things which were a matter of routine for him and he used to enjoy and would look forward to: one was going to the local church every Sunday morning to attend the mass and pray before the beautiful statue of Virgin Mary; and the other was standing by the side of his bedroom window at night before going to sleep and looking at the sky and murmuring as if he was talking to someone. His grandma used to think that he was talking to his deceased parents but then she wondered how could that be – he had never seen them as they died soon after his birth in a car accident.

For the previous few weeks, the speech and the physical therapists both were finding some positive change in Tommy. He looked happier and more cheerful. Then something happened suddenly one Sunday morning. When Grandma Susan woke up at 6.30 am, she found Tommy already totally dressed up, ready to go to the church. He even refused to take his light breakfast so impatient he was. Grandma Susan got ready fast and found Tommy waiting with her purse and the car keys.

When they arrived at the church, the cleaner John was cleaning up the premises. He was utterly surprised to see them arrive so early. Anyway, he allowed them to get in and take seats in the front row. The church hall was full with people and the mass started at 9 am sharp. Tommy was fully focussed and he was murmuring all the while. When the pastor finished his presentation, Tommy spoke with a clear voice. There was no stuttering or any affectation. He said: "The beautiful lady was speaking to me and I was speaking to her". He pointed towards the statue of Virgin Mary. The eyes of all the people who had assembled were looking towards the child full of wonder. Tommy went on saying very distinctly: "She taught me the prayer and she told me not to worry. She said, she will remain with me always!" The whole assembly was stunned.

Virgin Mary miraculously cured an autistic boy and made him speak which was unbelievable. Such was her grace!! *(Reference 1)*

A Non-religious Young Man's Dream to Know About the Brain

Dr Michael Egnor, MD was born into a kind of non-religious family as a child and he fell in love with science at a very early age. And he thought that all the mysteries of life, all the really meaningful things, that one could discover could be discovered through science. So, he believed in the Darwinian way of understanding man, and physics and chemistry and all those things.

He majored in biochemistry in college and wanted to be a doctor. And, he wanted to be a neurosurgeon because he wanted to understand the brain and the mind. He thought that if he could understand on a deep level who we were and what we were if he knew all the science there was to know about the brain. So, he graduated from the medical school. He trained in neurosurgery and graduated from his residency in 1991 and went out and practiced as a neurosurgeon.

And a number of things happened to him as a neurosurgeon and as a husband and as a father that changed the way he looked at the world.

A Fresh Neurosurgeon Exposed to Brain Wonders

As a neurosurgeon, he began finding patients who had large parts of their brains missing. A good example was a little girl who was born with only about half her brain. He told the girl's family that it did not look good. He couldn't be sure how she would eventually turn out. It didn't look encouraging. But, amazingly, the girl is now in her mid-20s and she is a normal, vibrant young woman, having a great job. Her mother told Dr Egnor that she was too smart for her own good, despite having only half a brain.

He had a number of patients with major parts of their brains missing but they were really OK – were really fine, no complaints. And, that didn't fit any of the neuroanatomy textbooks that he had read in medical school. There was a gap between theory and practice. There were strange things going on there. The whole thing kind of came to a head when he was operating, many years ago, on a woman who had a brain tumour in her brain's *left frontal lobe*. The functions of this part of the brain include: processing speech and language, enabling verbal communication, supporting logical thinking, executive functions like problem-solving, decision-making, working memory and planned and goal-directed behaviour – for a right-handed person. He was performing an 'Awake Brain Surgery' on this patient. Pioneered by Dr Wilder Penfield at McGill University, Canada, in the late 1920s and 1930s, in this procedure, the patient is given a local anaesthetic so he didn't feel the pain. The brain tissue itself has no sensation of pain. So, it's just like cutting the hair. You don't feel anything. And, the surgical team can stimulate the surface of the exposed brain and get a map of the critical parts of the brain. So, for example, if the surgeon is removing a tumour, he can find out what portions of the tissue he has to protect and what other portions he can safely remove to get the tumour out with minimum damage to any critical function. So, the procedure makes the operation safer. So, the patient lady was awake and Dr Egnor was working on the tumour and taking out much of the *left frontal lobe* of her brain, while having a conversation. And, it was a perfectly normal conversation despite the fact that a large chunk was removed. The surgical action and its end-result did not seem to make any difference in the patient's conversation. Fortunately, the whole point of surgery was to keep her healthy and as much normal as possible.

There are 'eloquent' and 'non-eloquent' areas of the human brain. Eloquent areas are regions critical for specific, readily identifiable neurological functions like movement, speech, and vision, and their injury leads to disabling deficits. Non-eloquent areas, conversely, are regions where damage does not cause a severe or permanent functional loss, or where the function is more subtle to identify. Dr Egnor started wondering if some non-eloquent areas of the patient's brain were automatically taking over the functions of the surgically removed eloquent areas. He was totally puzzled. After a few such puzzling experiences he thought, goodness gracious, we don't understand what the brain does. There must be something deeper here. Because none of his textbooks had said that you could take out most of the *left frontal lobe* and have a person to be totally normal.

A Religious Conversion

At the same time, Dr Egnor had a religious conversion, one might say. And, it was related intellectually to some of his doubts about Darwinism. He started reading more deeply about the Darwinian explanation for how we became human, and it struck him as pretty weak science. He just thought that of all the scientific disciplines he had known, this was the one that he thought was least rigorous.

Dr Egnor had four kids, and when his youngest son was born, for the first couple of months of his life, he wasn't making eye contact, and he wasn't smiling. He wasn't behaving as if he understood his mom and dad to be living people. They were mere objects to him. Dr Egnor became frightened that he was 'autistic'; and 'autism' had always terrified him. The idea that you have a child – your own child whom you love and want to connect with and it doesn't even know that you exist. How pathetic! You're just like a piece of furniture to the infant. Dr Egnor took him to some neurologists and, they said, he was too young – just a 2–3 months' old; you really can't be sure.

So, by the time he was almost six months old and still wasn't making eye contact, wasn't really interacting with, Dr Egnor went to consult a specialist at an outside multi-speciality hospital. It was a Catholic set-up. He was at a point where he was emotionally really distraught. He was thinking that he was never going to have his son love him. The boy was never going to know him. So, after he and his wife had seen the consultant, it was quite late at night. There was a chapel in the hospital. Dr Egnor made his wife and the child wait in the visitors' lounge and he stepped into the chapel.

He got down in front of the altar and prayed. And, he said: "God, I don't know if you exist. I have never made praying a habit. But, if you do exist, could you take this problem away from me please? This is something I cannot deal with. I can't have my son to be autistic and don't know me."

God Spoke to Him

And, he heard a voice, only time in his life, he'd ever heard a voice, and it was very clear, and it wasn't him saying it. And, the voice said: "But that's what you are doing to me. Are you not autistic towards me?"

Dr Egnor kind of collapsed and said: "Okay, I won't do it to you anymore. I won't be autistic to you. But please make my son no-autistic towards me."

He went home and a few days later was his son's six-month birthday and he was perfectly normal. He was perfectly fine. He is now grown up, studying law and is anything but autistic.

So, that complemented in some sense Dr Egnor's discoveries as a surgeon and in neuroscience, that there is a lot more than just meat – that we do have *souls*, that there is a spiritual aspect to us.

Conversion to Christianity

Dr Egnor and his whole family got converted to Christianity, and got baptized. And, since he had spent several decades of his life as an atheist and a materialist, he kind of felt that he has a debt to repay. *(Reference 2)*

[When a newly born child exchanges positive eye contact and smile with the mother, it is expressing its GRATITUDE most subtly for allowing its SOUL to enter and develop in the protected shelter of her womb. When it exchanges positive eye contact and smile with the father, it is expressing its GRATITUDE most subtly for having contributed equally with its mother in its creation. If the child does not show such signs of GRATITUDE, it is taken as suffering from AUTISM.]

Hearing Voices (Auditory Hallucination)

'*Inner speech*' is a pre-requisite of all voluntary activity. One talks to himself quietly in the mind the whole day prior to and post-every action. This is absolutely normal. But when in danger, he hears an inner voice that is wholly unlike the normal babble of inner speech.

The great Russian psychologist Lev Vygotsky had a great struggle crossing a stream with an injured knee. He says: "The effort left me stunned, motionless for a couple of minutes, and then a delicious languor came over me, and I thought to myself – why not rest here? ....This was immediately countered by a strong, clear, commanding voice, which said – 'You can't rest here – you can't rest anywhere. You've got to go on. Find a pace you can keep up and go on steadily'. This good voice, this live voice, braced and resolved me. I stopped trembling and did not falter again".

Such voices may occur with anyone in situations of *extreme stress.* Sigmund Freud also had heard such voices on two occasions.

Various explanations have been offered for why people hear voices. Auditory hallucination may be associated with abnormal activation of the primary auditory cortex. However, this is a subject that needs much more investigation as it takes place not only in the case of psychotics and schizophrenics but in the population at large.

Some researchers have proposed that auditory hallucinations result from a failure to recognise internally generated speech as one's own. It may also stem from a cross-activation with the auditory areas. Perhaps there is some sort of physiological barrier that normally prevents most of us from *hearing* such 'inner voices' as external. Perhaps that barrier is somehow undeveloped in those who do hear constant voices. Nevertheless, we should try to get a concrete answer to the question: why most of us do not *hear voices*?

I will soon be introducing you to Julian Jaynes who, in his influential 1976 book *The Origin of Consciousness in the Breakdown of the Bicameral Mind*, speculated that, not so long ago, all humans *heard voices* – generated internally from the right hemisphere of the brain, but perceived (by the left hemisphere) as if external, and taken as direct communication from gods. Sometimes, around 1,000 BC, Jaynes proposed, with the rise of modern consciousness, the voices became internalised and recognised as the hearer's own.

Invasion by 'Dark Energy' ('*Krishna Shakti*')

Jeffrey John Kripal is the J. Newton Rayzor Chair in Philosophy and Religious Thought at Rice University in Houston, Texas, USA. In his late-teens and early-twenties, he attended a seminary. In 1981 when Jeff was 18, he entered and in 1985 at the age of 22, he left the seminary. This was the period when he was totally confused about certain Catholic practices. The confusion made him anorexic – deeply anorexic. He was also living in a religious community that was over a number of years he came to understand as primarily a gay community – not in any explicit or expressed way but in a kind of sublimated spiritual way. He himself was not a gay but he was deeply confused sexually and the anorexia was a part of that. Freud saved his life as otherwise he would have died out of starvation. The psychoanalyst, of course, helped him by making him understand Freud and his concepts.

When he left life at the seminary, he could not find any resources for a male heterosexual mystical life. There was no way to be a straight guy to be a Catholic Mystic because the Catholic Mystic is always called upon to marry Christ, which is a homeo-erotic thing if you happen to be a man. And Christ was the only God-like figure – there was no goddess. That is the dilemma in Catholicism; so, he was interested in Hinduism and Buddhism as there are all these goddesses which looked like a real resource for such a heterosexual mystical life – so that's what took him to graduate school and that is why he wrote his dissertation and his first book on the life of the Indian mystic Sri Sri Ramakrishna who, incidentally, used to cross dress and behave so much effeminately that it was difficult to make out whether he was a male or a female. This used to happen when the saint used to have *madhura bhava* – which is the frame of body as well as mind – a disposition when the individual develops the nature of Sri Radhika, the consort of Lord Krishna. Jeff had not known about this aspect of Ramakrishna's personality.

Jeff was working on a form of Hinduism called the *Shakti Tantra* – a tantric tradition very influential in West Bengal. It focuses around the Goddess Kali – it involves the presence of something called *Shakti* (Energy) – mystical energy which is also conscious. It was the fall of 1989 – autumn in West Bengal, during a festival called *Kali Puja* – series of days dedicated to the worship of the Mother Goddess. Jeff was in Kolkata to collect data for his research work.

During that Festival, he woke up one morning but he just couldn't move. He felt as if he was paralysed. While he was trying to figure out what had happened, a flow of *energy* came out of him or out of the room or from somewhere and started to engage him in all of those really profound ways and he thought he was being electrocuted actually. He thought he was dying – maybe having a heart attack. Nothing was clear and, then at one point, the *energy* just sort of imploded right into the heart region and Jeff had this kind of classic out-of-body experience. He struggled for some time to try to get back into his body and when he got back into the body he felt this conscious *energy* that was crossing through him was really the inspiration for the dissertation and his first book. He felt invaded by a mystic power, possessed or radiated by the Goddess's *shakti.*

To find out the correct interpretation of this experience, he wrote book after book on mystic and paranormal phenomena trying to figure out what this thing or this presence was until a few years ago, he came to the conclusion that this experience was designed to set him on certain fact-finding paths that he later went down so he sees it now as sort of an infinitely meaningful and not plausible not definable in any clear or final sense – and he also doesn't try to. He has failed completely to get it back. As he himself was not capable of causing it in the first place, he can't get it back. So, he has to let it go and be at peace without it.

Actually, since Jeff was searching for a heterosexual mysticism so he needed a divine feminine and he got a glimpse of that kind of personal relationship.

My interpretation is that Goddess Kali's *shakti* is 'Dark Energy' ('*Krishna Shakti*') radiating from the 'Dark Matter' ('*Krishna Bastu*') from her dark basalt stone image. 'Dark Energy' is invisible and it can pass through the human body in a 'subtle' or a 'gross' way. When it passes in a 'gross' way, you feel the presence of the energy as if you're electrocuted, and you may have 'out-of-the-body' experience. This might have had happened to Jeff Kripal which made him realise that *shakti* is real, not imaginary. That is why the *Shakti Tantra* has gained firm ground in West Bengal.

[*Shakti Tantra* is a way of understanding and respecting the special feminine power in the world. It helps people see how the masculine and feminine energies inside us work together. When we understand this and make these work together, we stop seeing them as different and start seeing how they come together as one big energy.]

Goddess Kali's Laughter

The basalt stone form of Goddess Kali is meant for common religious people for whom 'Spirituality' is a distant domain. To understand the Real Goddess Kali, you have to go much beyond the rituals of religion. Goddess Kali, wearing a garland of skulls, symbolises *decay*. She symbolises *entropy* – randomness in the system, gradual decline into disorder. While other Gods like Brahma and Vishnu promise salvation through order, she exposes the truth, the reality through disorder. She is the heat death of the universe, with all its ambiguities and waste, turned into a mother figure. She reveals that every beginning carries its own end, like a seed ends up in the soil from where it had sprung into life. She turns galaxies into dust and dust into galaxies. Kali is what life resists and what life eventually becomes. The concept of Kali is linked with the cremation ground; and the laughter of Kali that enters into our ears in the cremation grounds should not be taken as most horrifying – it should be regarded as Kali's weird sense of humour.

Her dark skin symbolises 'infinity'. The protruded tongue is the mockery of our appetite for the short-term 'feel good' brain chemical 'Dopamine' ('D'). Our hunger for information can simply not be satiated permanently as, at every moment, we get flooded with some new information. So, the birth and death of information follow a cycle. In between, if there is a wrong information coming in, which is not authentic, the whole process gets disrupted. Onset of a disease is the incoming of wrong information – something alien to the process. This leads to disruption. Thakur Ramakrishna's throat cancer was one such event, but it very much represented reality. Not to be affected by such unprecedented crises, one must develop humility and sense of humour. An individual must be prepared to hear Kali's laughter at the moment of death. *(Reference 3)*

Goddess Came in His Dreams

Namagiri Devi, also known as Namagiri Thayar, is a Hindu goddess, particularly revered in the southern parts of India. She was the divine teacher of the renowned mathematician Srinivasa Ramanujan (1887–1920). Ramanujan attributed his groundbreaking mathematical insights to Namagiri Devi, believing she communicated complex formulas to him through dreams and visions which he would then verify through rigorous calculations to discover their authenticity. She is a form of goddess Lakhsmi and the consort of Narasimha. Ramanujan claimed that Namagiri Devi would etch mathematical formulas, such as infinite series, partitions, and modular forms, onto his mind during dreams. His devotion to Namagiri Devi was deeply ingrained in his life, and he would often visit her temple and sleep at the deity's feet. She is particularly revered at the Namakkal Narasimha Swamy Temple, where she is the main deity, granting prayers for prosperity, wisdom, and guidance.

Ramanujan's story highlights a profound connection between spirituality and mathematical truth, where divine revelations merged with the mathematical insight. His formulas are still used in modern advancements like black hole physics and quantum theory. Ramanujan used to say:

> "An equation for me has no meaning unless it expresses a thought of god". Ramanujan's mother was equally devoted to the goddess and, as the story goes, the goddess Namagiri had appeared in her dream and said that she was going to give birth to a child who would be a mathematical genius.

Mahadevi Akka's Chenna Mallikarjuna

Akka Mahadevi (1130–1160) was born in Udutadi, near Shivamogga in the State of Karnataka in South India. She was born to Nirmalshetti and Sumati – devotees of Lord Shiva. When she grew up, a local Jain King named Kaushika sought to marry her, but she rejected him as she was totally devoted to Lord Shiva.

She used to compose poems and circulate them, and in one of her poems, she had laid down three conditions for marrying the King, including control over the choice to spend her time in devotion or in conversation with other scholars and religious figures than with the King. Such conditions were not acceptable to the King, so the marriage did not occur. This is one account. According to another account, the marriage took place but King Kaushika violated the conditions she had laid down, so Mahadevi left the palace, leaving all her possessions including clothes, to travel to Srisailam, home of the god Parama Shiva. Alternative accounts suggest that Akka Mahadevi's act of renunciation was a response to King's threats after she refused his proposal. She is believed to have travelled towards the end of her trip to the Srisailam shrine where she lived as an ascetic and eventually died. One of her poems suggests that towards the end of her life, King Kaushika visited her there and sought her forgiveness.

She wrote that she was a woman only in name and that her mind, body, and soul had belonged to Lord Shiva. In search of her soulmate Lord Shiva, she made animals, flowers and birds her friends and companions, rejecting family life and worldly attachment. Her poetry explores the rejection of mortal love in favour of the love of God. The seeker should kill the 'I', conquer desires and the senses.

An ascetic, Mahadevi is said to have refused to wear any clothing. Legend has it that due to true love and devotion with God her whole body was protected by Him.

One of her famous *vachanas* is translated as:

> "People male and female
> Blush when a cloth covering the shame comes loose
> When the Lord of lives
> lives drowned without a face
> in the world, how can you be modest?
>
> When all the world is the eye of the Lord
> on looking everywhere, what can you
> cover and conceal?"

The direct and frank lyrics that Akka Mahadevi wrote have been described as embodying a 'radical illegitimacy' that reexamines the role of women as actors with volition and will, behaving in opposition to established social institutions and mores. At times, she uses strong sexual imagery to represent the unison between the devotee and the object of devotion. Her works challenge common understandings of sexual identity, for instance, in one *vachana* she suggests that creation, or the power of the God Shiva is masculine, while all creation, including men, represent the feminine. "I saw the haughty master Mallikarjuna for whom men, all men, are but women, wives. In some *vachanas*, she describes herself as both feminine and masculine.

One of the most moving uses of the extended analogue is Mahadevi Akka's love of God, where all the phases of love become metaphors. For instance:

> "I have Maya for mother-in-law;
> the world would be father-in-law;
> three brothers-in-laws like tigers;
> and the husband's thoughts
> are full of laughing women;
> no god, this man
>
> And I cannot cross the sister-in-law.
> But, I will give this wench the slip
> and go cuckold my husband with Hara, my lord.
> My mind is my maid, by her kindness, I join my Lord.
> my utterly beautiful Lord, from the mountain peaks
> my lord as white as jasmine
> and I will make Him
> my good husband."

In this *vachana*, she is an 'abhisharika' – a woman stealing out of a houseful of relatives to meet her lover, is the central image. The method is the method of allegory, explicitly equating, one-for-one, various members of the household, with various abstractions: *Maya* or 'Primal Illusion' is the mother-in-law, the world is the father-on-law. The three brothers-in-law, are the three *gunas*, which keep a tiger-vigil. The husband is *Karma*, the past of the ego's many lives. The ritualistic law, who also keeps the speaker imprisoned in apparently the *vasana*, the binding memory or 'smell' that the 'Karma-Past' carries with it. The kind of confidants or maid is the *Mind*, who alone helps her meet the Lord and keep the tryst.

The relationships mentioned here are all made by 'marriage', Not a single person is related to the woman by birth. This elaborate build-up of social bonds is shattered by the cuckolding climax of the poem, with the Lord as the adulterous lover. Elsewhere also, Mahadeviyakka rejects outright all notions of modesty as a virtue. She is supposed to have thrown off her clothes; at one point, in defiance of the indecent pruderies of the society around her. This shows 'Love of God' as 'anti-structure', 'anti-social', 'unruly' relationship – an act of violation against ordinary expected loyalties – a breakdown of the predictable and the secure. *(References 4-6)*

God's Chosen Servant Leader

Moses presents an excellent model for the study of biblical *servant leadership* in the Old Testament, for which the essential qualities are: compassion, humility, altruism, stewardship, and service of others. Although far from perfect, there are ample stories from Moses's life that point to the motivations and virtues of his leadership as well as the antecedents and outcomes of Moses's behaviour as a leader. A servant leader's motivation is to 'serve first' and cause the overflow of that desire into action that empowers others.

Moses was not like this all along. The first forty years of his life were spent in royal comfort and style in the Pharaoh's palace in Cairo, Egypt. The next forty years of his life were spent in a shepherd community in the forest land of Egypt. When Moses was 80 years old, God appeared to him in the form of a 'burning bush'. Moses could not have delivered Israelites out of Egypt, and sustained them in the wilderness 40 years, without the direct miraculous help of God. This high privilege was accompanied by almost unbelievable suffering. Aside from Jesus, it has never been given to any man to be agent of so many stupendous manifestations of Divine power.

God, often referred to as the Lord (Yahweh) gave Moses the power to perform miracles, such as turning his staff into a snake and making his hand leprous and then healing it, to convince the Israelites and Pharaoh that he was God's chosen messenger. These powers and many more were granted to Moses by divine authority to serve as signs and to demonstrate God's sovereignty and power over the Egyptians. The power began when God appeared to Moses in the 'burning bush' on Mount Horeb, calling him to take the leadership to deliver the Israelites from slavery in Egypt. Moses was initially hesitant and felt inadequate, but God provided him with these signs as a sign of His support and power. These were intended to serve as a proof of God's presence and authority to both the Israelites and Pharaoh. Later, God specifically instructed Moses to "perform before Pharaoh all the miracles I have put in your power", indicating the divine source of the ability to perform these wonders.

Jesus Blinded Paul with Bright Light

Paul (c. 5 – c. 64/65 AD) lived as a Pharisee, and participated in the persecution of early disciples of Lord Jesus. On his way to arrest Christians in Damascus, Paul suddenly saw a bright light which blinded him and he heard Jesus call him by his Jewish name 'Saul'. Jesus asked him why he was against him and his disciples. He explained to him what his mission was and sent his disciple Ananias from Damascus to restore his sight. When his sight was restored, Paul got convinced and baptized. Soon thereafter, he began to proclaim that Jesus of Nazareth was the Jewish Messiah and the Son of God. He made three missionary journeys to spread the Christian message to non-Jewish communities during the 1st century.

Later known as St. Paul, he was not one of Jesus's Twelve Apostles, and he did not meet Jesus face to face during his lifetime but had experienced his super powers and knew about his teachings. *(References 7-16)*

References

1. "5-year-Old Boy with Autism NEVER Spoke, When Seeing Virgin Mary, Something Shocking Happened", Video Presentation on You Tube, *Miracles of Mary Channel*, September 2025.
2. "Neurosurgeon Converts to Christianity After This Happens". Video Presentation on YouTube, *Aspiring Christian Channel*, 25th June 2025.
3. Partha Sinha, "Kali and The Wisdom of Entropy", *The Times of India, Kolkata Edition,* 13th November 2025, p. 14.
4. 'Akka Mahadevi' – *Wikipedia.*
5. *Speaking of Siva*, Translated with an Introduction by A.K. Ramanujan, Middlesex, England: Penguin Books, 1985.

6. "Scribbles on Akka" – maDHusree duTTa, madhusreedutta.net
7. Oliver Sacks, *Hallucinations*, New York & Toronto: Alfred A. Knopf, 2012.
8. "The Erotic and Esoteric in Religion with Jeffrey Kripal" Video Presentation on You Tube, *New Thinking Allowed* with Jeffrey Mishlove (4K Reboot), February 2025.
9. "Shakti Tantra – The Union of Energies", *Himalayan Yoga Ashram.*
10. Magdalena Hau, "The Role of Shakti Tantra", *Tara Yoga a Tantra Spirituality*, 24th August 2022.
11. "Namagiri" – *Wikipedia.*
12. "The Goddess of Ramanujan's Akashic Dreams" # namagiri # nationalmathematicsday# india# dreamyoga. You Tube video presentation.
13. "Moses" – *Wikipedia.*
14. "The Miracles of Moses" – Journey through the New Testament with Us, *The Free Bible Lessons Center – Halley's Bible Handbook*, Grand Rapids, Michigan: Zondervan Publishing House.
15. "Empowering Stewardship: Leadership Lessons from Exodus 18": 13–27, *Regent University, USA.*
16. "Paul the Apostle" – *Wikipedia.*

CHAPTER 3

Only on God

Only on God

Ram Dass (1931–2019), also known as Baba Ram Dass, was born in Boston, Mass., USA, as Richard Alpert. A former professor of psychology at Harvard University, Ram Das was a spiritual teacher and guru of modern yoga and writer. His best-selling 1971 book is *Be Here Now*.

Alpert left his professor's job at Harvard, travelled to India and became a disciple of the Hindu guru Neem Karoli Baba in North India. Ram Dass was the name given to Richard by his guru. Once he was having *darshan* of his guru in his ashram and there were a few foreigners and several Indians who were visiting to get Karoli Baba's blessings. Amongst the Indian visitors, the Chief Justice of the Allahabad High Court was also present. When Karoli Baba introduced Ram Dass to all who were present, the Chief Justice invited Ram Dass to visit the Allahabad High Court as his guest. Ram Dass requested him to take the Guru's permission. The Guru didn't object – he gave his consent immediately.

In the Allahabad High Court, all the judges and senior lawyers, when they met Ram Dass, wanted to know his views on the then US President Richard Nixon's foreign policy. Ram Dass was taken a little aback as he had expected them to ask him about his impression about Hinduism. He was surprised that there was never a mention about that topic in course of their 2-hour long meeting. When Ram Dass talked to Karoli Baba on his such experience in the High Court, the Guru didn't speak, he only smiled.

On the very next day, another Allahabad High Court lawyer wanted Ram Dass to address the Rotary Club of Allahabad and also the Bar Association of Allahabad. When Neem Karoli Baba asked the lawyer gentleman on what topic he would like Ram Dass to talk to those gatherings. The lawyer promptly said: "On Nixon's foreign policy, of course! We want to hear about that from an American himself."

Neem Karoli Baba promptly responded displaying a smart smile on his face: "I'm extremely sorry! Ram Dass speaks **ONLY ON GOD**! He does not speak on any other topic. Speaking on any other topic will disturb his mind's spiritual ambience which has been tuned to a very high frequency. Talking about politics, foreign policy and even about your own family and household will lower his mental frequency – which is forbidden for a *bhakta*, for a *sadhak*." The matter ended there! *(Reference 1)*

Decorating God with Passion

In the slopes of Tirumala in South India, there was a flower merchant called Pandaram. He had a son called Anandan. Pandaram had a lot of flowers growing around his house. His son used to help him every day. Father taught Anandan to mix flowers and make beautiful garlands. Chanting Lord Krishna's name, he learned how to make the best garlands. Even though it was his livelihood, he always did his work with the aim of **decorating God.** From childhood to adulthood, passing through the teens, he continued his chants and daily chores.

Anandan got up very early in the morning every day and, as he started his work, he got engaged totally. Once his garlands were made, he went to the Papanasam river behind his hut for a dip, came back and put on the clothes he had hung to dry. Then he would start climbing the hill to meet God.

One morning, he was collecting flowers when something bit him. He was least bothered, totally unfazed – he continued his work. Suddenly a sound echoed in the background. "My dear devotee", the voice said, "I think you have been bitten by a snake...".

Anandan, busy plucking flowers, swayed his head, in confirmation without stopping his work.

"Are you not afraid?", the voice asked.
"I don't know if it is poisonous, so I'm not afraid", Anandan said.
"What if it is?", the voice echoed again.

Prompt came Anandan's reply: "If it is not, I'll meet you in the temple. And, if it is, then I'll meet you in Vaikuntha – your heavenly abode."

Anandan's confidence made Lord Krishna spellbound.

This story is about Anandan, a famous devotee of Lord Vishnu. The story shows how Anandan was unmoved by the fear of his death as his brain was in the FLOW state, equivalent to *savikalpa samadhi.* It was because of the fact that his 'True Passion' (devotion to God) had merged with his 'Profession' (making beautiful garlands with a variety of flowers to offer to God). His confidence and dedication had made God's blessings to be present with him always and he could feel the presence of God as *Sound Energy*.

The Eating God

The story of the Alarnath Temple centres on the legend of Lord Jagannath manifesting as a four-armed deity, Alarnath, during the Anavasara period, which is when the main Jagannath idol is being replaced and unavailable for *darshan*.

A priest, named Sri Ketan lived with his son Madhu in the temple and they only consumed the prasad after it has been ceremonially offered to the deity. The deity being a stone idol naturally did not touch the prasad; it used to remain intact.

One day, Sri Ketan had to travel on work and he asked his wife to prepare the kheer (milk and rice) and get Madhu to offer it to God. Madhu had initially refused because he did not have the confidence as he was not aware of the rituals, the mantras and so on, but finally agreed when his parents explained to him that nothing wrong will happen. He need not follow any rituals; he only had to take the bowl and place it before the God with devotion.

Madhu followed the instructions, left the bowl in front of the deity and then went to play his friends. When he came back, he found that God has not taken anything; the bowl was just as it was before, filled with the prasad. Madhu got very upset, started crying and enquired if he had done anything wrong. God was touched by Madhu's sincerity, manifested himself and consumed the whole prasad, leaving nothing for Sri Ketan's family. Sri Ketan's wife was furious with Madhu as she thought that Madhu had eaten it all up and he was lying.

Meanwhile, Sri Ketan came back. He asked his wife to prepare kheer and told Madhu to take the bowl and offer it to God. Sri Ketan was hiding himself behind a curtain. And, what he saw was totally unbelievable. When Madhu offered the bowl to God and most sweetly asked him to take it, God manifested himself and as he was about to consume the prasad from the bowl, Sri Ketan ran to the living God and tried to snatch the bowl from his hand. In the process, the hot prasad fell on God's body and he got slight burns. Sri Ketan said: "Oh, Lord! If you consume the whole prasad, what will be left for us?"

Lord said: "The prasad is prepared for whom – for me or for you and the family? I've not been eating it all these days because I was aware of your selfish motive and nobody offered me with unselfish love and unconditional devotion. When you offer me anything, you always want something in return. Innocent and pure-natured Madhu did not ask any favour from me. He was totally unselfish and, that is the reason, I took the prasad from him and ate it up. Is it clear now?"

In Bhagavad Gita, Lord Krishna says: "If one offers Me with love and devotion a leaf, a flower, a fruit, water, I will accept it. The most important is the love and devotion that is carried through the food to the gods".

The burn marks manifested by Lord Alarnath are still visible on the deity's body. *(References 2&3)*

Can Microbes Be Our Gods

John Cryan of the University of Cork, Ireland, and his colleagues have been working to ascertain the possibility that the microbial communities living outside and inside our bodies in widely spread colonies may act more like puppet masters we, the civilised mammals being the puppets in their hands. They describe how microbes can dramatically affect brain function and behaviour. Exactly, who is in charge, our microbiome or our mammalian self, remains an open question.

Cryan and his team and other dedicated scientists in other continents are exploring the possibility of providing *Sustained Happiness* to patients of psychosis including paranoid schizophrenia by trying out 'faecal transplantation', where the 1st step is to ascertain the patient's gut microbial status and identify which microbes are lacking, and then, in the 2nd step, to insert the microbes in the form of 'faecal transplants'. The results so far are most encouraging and if it really works, then microbes will be our Gods. *(Reference 4)*

References

1. "Only God – Ram Dass Tell A Maharaj Ji Story (Rare Uncovered Archives)/90's" – Video Presentation on You Tube, *Baba Ram Dass Channel.*
2. "Alarnatha Mandira" – *Wikipedia.*
3. Mehul Vora, "A God Who Burnt His Hand" – *Scriptwallah.*
4. Rodney Dietert, *The Human Super-organism: How the Microbiome is Revolutionizing the Pursuit of Healthy Life*, New York: Dutton, 2016, p. 65.

CHAPTER 4

God: Where are You

Longing for the Invisible God

Is there some way I can reach you?
You have no end and no beginning.

I want to praise your good qualities,
but you have no qualities,
I try to think you in my mind
You sit behind every thought.

Is there some way I can reach you?
I want to worship you with my hands,
but you are huge, you fill all space
I would bring you a gift, but you have
everything in the world

Is there some way I can reach you?
I want to see you with my eyes
You have no visible form.
God on the hill, you're in all these things,
All I can say, I am yours.
Is there some way I can reach you?

***(Poet:** Annamacharya 1408–1503, Telugu musician, composer of 'samkirtanas' and Hindu saint; Translators: V. Narayana Rao and David Shulman)*

From: *A Book of Bhakti Poetry: Eating God*; Ed: Arundhati Subramaniam, London: Penguin)

Gods & Goddesses with Multiple Heads and Arms

There are four lobes in each hemisphere of the brain: two frontal, two temporal, two parietal, and two occipital. So, there are altogether eight lobes in the whole brain. The four lobes in the left hemisphere have different functions from the corresponding ones in the right hemisphere. In ancient times, the scholars of religious studies had no knowledge about the well laid-out structure and multiple functions of the human brain, but based on their 'gut feelings', they had developed the concept of gods and goddesses with multiple heads and arms, but having only two legs.

Gods and goddesses with multiple heads are prominent figures in various mythologies. In Hinduism, we have Brahma (four heads), Kartikeya/Subramanya (six heads), Ganesha (five heads), Dattatreya (three heads), and sometimes Shiva and Saraswati are also depicted with multiple heads.

Brahma is the creator god with four heads, symbolising the four Vedas, or different aspects of consciousness. Dattatreya is an *avatar* of Trimurti, represented with three heads, symbolising Brahma, Vishnu, and Shiva. Kartikeya/Subramanya is the god of war, often shown with six heads, symbolising the six faces he had at birth. Ganesha's each head represents one of the five sheaths (or *koshas*). Agni, the god of fire, has two heads. Shiva sometimes is depicted with five heads, often representing the five states of consciousness. Saraswati, the goddess of knowledge, is sometimes depicted with multiple arms, and occasionally associated with multiple heads.

Multiple heads can represent a divine being's comprehensive understanding, the ability to see, hear, and understand things on a superhuman level, or various forms of their power. They can also signify being beyond the constraints of time or the totality of creation, as in the case of Brahma.

In Hinduism, deities are often depicted with multiple arms, which they use for battling with cosmic forces. We, humans, have two arms and a divided brain to battle with the forces in our environment.

In Egyptian-inspired Greek esoteric writings connected with Hermes Trismegistus, Hecate is described as having three heads: one dog, one serpent, and one horse. In other representations, her animal heads include those of a cow and a boar.

Visible Demi-gods

Ancient humans did realise that God is an entity beyond perception as he was all-pervasive and invisible. So, they created visible *demi-gods.* Ancient Greek demi-gods were legendary figures, children of god and a mortal, possessing extraordinary abilities and often becoming great heroes. Notable examples include: Heracles (son of Zeus), Achilles (son of the sea nymph Thetis), and Perseus (son of Zeus), who were known for their incredible strengths and heroic deeds. The concept of demi-gods was also used to explain the origins of heroes and bridge the gap between the mortal and immortal realms.

The concept of demi-gods in ancient Egypt is questionable and not a core element of their original mythology. However, some historical figures like Imhotep, a renowned architect and physician, have been identified as potential demi-gods, particularly by later Hellenistic cultures. Egyptians never believed in the idea of gods physically procreating with humans to produce demi-gods.

In Hindu mythology, Nandi, Garuda, Madurai Veeran and Karuppu Sami (or Karuppusamy) are examples of demi-gods. Karuppusamy is known as the 'black god' and is considered a protector, healer, and god of justice. Devotees seek his intervention for various afflictions and protection from evil.

Monotheistic religions like Judaism, Christianity and Islam have only one God. Can we say that in these religions, their principal prophets: Abraham and Moses in Judaism, Jesus in Christianity, and Muhammad in Islam can be regarded as demi-gods as much as the *avatars* like Chaitanya Mahaprabhu and Sri Sri Ramakrishna Paramhansa in Hinduism?

Demi-gods had physical existence and their voices could also be heard when they were present on this planet.

Omnipresent, omnipotent, omniscient God is invisible, but His voice can be heard as you will read below.

God Inside the Human Body

The Bauls (singing minstrels) of India's West Bengal and Bangladesh have always claimed that the 'Cosmos' (*Brahmanda*) is in the 'Human Body' (*Deha Bhanda*). There is no doubt that the human body is God's marvellous creation. There is an exclusive section of Baul songs, titled as 'Songs of the Body' (*Deha Tattver Gaan*). Let me give you some remarkable examples from human biology.

Amongst the life-sustaining involuntary biological cycles in the body, the *cardiac cycle* is a principal one. It is the performance of the human heart from the beginning of one heart beat to the beginning of the next. It consists of two periods: one during which the heart muscle relaxes and refills with blood, called *diastole*, following a period of robust contraction and pumping of blood, called *systole*. After emptying, the heart relaxes and expands, to receive another influx of blood returning from the lungs and other systems of the body, before again contracting.

[As the myth goes, Lord Sri Krishna's living heart was transplanted into Lord Jagannath's chest. Known as *brahma vastu*, it used to be taken out during the deity's *snan yatra*.]

Another most crucial handiwork of biology is the *respiratory cycle*. It is the complete process of breathing in and out and consists of: (i) Inspiration (Inhalation) – active phase where air enters as an input into the lungs; (ii) Expiratory Pause – a very brief amount of rest after the inhalation is complete so that the inhaled air gets distributed all over the place; (iii) Expiration (Exhalation) – this is the phase where the air leaves the lungs so that no residue is left; (iv) Inspiratory Pause – a brief amount of rest before the next inhalation begins.

During inspiration, muscles like the *diaphragm* contract, increasing the thoracic cavity's volume and decreasing alveolar pressure to force air out of the lungs.

Respiration is primarily an involuntary activity, but it can also be temporarily controlled voluntarily. The *brainstem* portion of the *hindbrain* automatically regulates breathing to ensure exchange of gases, even during sleep or unconsciousness.

[Avatar Sri Sri Ramakrishna's mother Goddess Kali used to breathe as Thakur used to test her by holding a piece of fine cloth near the deity's nose.]

These two cases, Lord Krishna's living heart inside Lord Jagannath's chest and Thakur Ramakrishna's respirating Goddess Kali, indicate that such biological processes are God's golden gifts to us, humans.

Amongst other paired organs of vital importance inside the body, we have two kidneys. However, neither kidney is inherently more important. They are fundamentally equivalent, both performing the vital function of filtering blood removing waste and maintaining the body's fluid balance, although there are a few trivial structural differences which have no impact on their overall function. The body relies on the combined effect of both kidneys for proper health.

There is one *adrenal gland* on top of each kidney.

Females have two ovaries, and males two testes. Both have two breasts.

God Inside the Human Brain

Talking about the biology of the human brain, we know that its two halves – the left and the right hemisphere are not identical. While they are roughly symmetrical at a macroscopic level, they exhibit subtle structural, functional, and chemical asymmetries that allow for specialised cognitive tasks.

In pre-historic times, when the human brain was not as developed as it is today, one could most simplistically imagine that the human mind had two chambers, equivalent to the two hemispheres of the brain. Late Professor Jujian Jaynes (1920–1997) of Princeton University had based his concept of the *Bicameral Mind* on these two hemispheres, each representing one chamber. For right-handed people, the left hemisphere was considered responsible for all the day-to-day routine activities – physical, social, and mental for day-to-day living and working. The left brain was the 'executing' or 'output-producing' tissue and everything, all its functions, was being carried out totally *unconsciously* like automatons. Whenever there used to be a non-routine, novel situation – a problem or a crisis, the right hemisphere used to send instructions, advices and commands across to the left brain through the inter-connecting commissures or tissues. And the people used to believe that those were the acts of God. So, God had His existence inside the man himself.

The *Bicameral Mind*, with its inter-hemispheric verbal communication lost its value in general with the advent of written scripts and when single-cultured small tribal habitations got transformed into bi-cultural or tri-cultural towns and, thereafter, cities with people from different cultures speaking and writing in different languages. That was the time when, according to Jaynes, *consciousness* and *volition* developed in humans.

However, it is not true that the human mind has seized to function in the *bicameral* way as in the pre-historic era. Even the modern brain still adopts the ancient strategy under acute *stress* as I have shown in the above two cases.

'Bicameral Mind' may experience all kinds of sensory hallucination: Visual (seeing someone); Auditory (listening to a voice, or chant or music); Olfactory (getting a beautiful fragrance); Gustatory (getting the taste of nectar); Tactile & Proprioceptive (feeling a divine power touching/putting pressure on the whole body on the surface and all the parts).

Dr Egnor had auditory hallucination whereas Dr Kripal had tactile and proprioceptive hallucination. Kripal's hallucinatory experience was so intense that he was compelled to leave his gross body on the bed under the unbearable pressure and move his subtle body out to have an 'Out of the Body' experience.

Can you claim that your mind is like COSMOS which is in perfect order, or is it in utter disorderly CHAOS? Your *Bicameral Mind* operates when your mind is in utter disorderly *CHAOS*, to set it right – to help you to develop it like the orderly *COSMOS*.

The 'Divided' Brain

Birds and animals also have 'divided' brains. A bird needs to be able, for example, to pick out a seed against the background of tiny particles of stone or sand, to pick up a particular twig to build its nest, and so on. For doing so, it must be focussed. But, if that is the only *attention* it is paying, it will soon end up as someone else's lunch, because it needs at the same time to pay a quite different type of attention to the world around it – a broad, open, sustained vigilance. How to pay such contrary type of *attention* to the world at once? Can *consciousness* be committed to two kinds of *attention* simultaneously? The solution appears to have been in the 'divided' brain – in brain's two separate hemispheres.

As a matter of fact, the brain tissue in each hemisphere is sufficient in itself and on its own to sustain *consciousness.* And since *attention* is an aspect of *consciousness*, each hemisphere can therefore attend to the world in a different way. The *consciousness* thus moves back and forth between the two hemispheres seamlessly, drawing on each as required, and often very rapidly.

For in humans, too, it turns out the hemispheres pay different types of *attention* to the world in a different way or with a different set of priorities and values: the left – to get and grasp and take for our own use with the help of the right hand; the right – to explore in the external world and collect information to facilitate the function of the left by transmitting the information through the connecting tissue. The right hemisphere underwrites sustained attention and vigilance for whatever may be, without preconception. Its *attention* is not in the service of day-to-day sustenance but in the service of connection and exploration for medium and long-term survival.

Neuro-psychiatrist Iain McGilchrist, who talks about the 'Divided Brain' in the new edition of his book *The Master and His Emissary: The Divided Brain and the Making of the Western World* tells a story of a wise, spiritual master whose domain grew so large that he had to delegate to his emissaries. One emissary became arrogant, thought he was wiser than his master, and usurped his power, ultimately leading the domain to ruin. McGilchrist applies this story to the human brain, seeing the right hemisphere as the 'Master' and the left hemisphere as the 'Emissary'. The human socio-economic environment became so materialistic that the left hemisphere overpowered the right hemisphere and science and technology, systems and procedures replaced all the intuitiveness, creativity, and flowing qualities of the right hemisphere. This left brain dominance has stripped the world of depth, colour and value, resulting in a less insightful and more unbalanced approach to reality.

The right hemisphere (Master) represents a broader, more flexible, and insightful view of the world, akin to the wise, patient master in the story. The left hemisphere (Emissary), is characterized by a narrower, more analytical focus on details, representing the ambitious and tyrant emissary. McGilchrist argues that this imbalance between the two hemispheres has profoundly shaped Western philosophy, culture, and thought since the time of Plato.

I find an echo of McGilchrist's notion in Julian Jaynes's concept of the breakdown of the *bicameral mind* where the god's voice-hearing input-generating right hemisphere had to give way the output-producing left hemisphere.

The terms 'Apollonian' and 'Dionysian' were introduced by Friedrich Nietszhe, the German philosopher to describe the two fundamental drives in human nature and culture. The term 'Apollonian' embodies reason, order, individuality and generally unperturbed calm, while the term 'Dionysian' represents instinct, emotion, lack of balance, and ecstatic-collective experience. Nietzsche argued that classical Greek tragedy arose from the tension and synthesis of these two forces. He firmly believed that both were necessary for a complete understanding of the human condition and the creation of great art.

Although in ancient Greece, there was no knowledge about the functions of the human brain, we find an analogy with the 'Divided Brain' concept – 'Apollonian' representing the left hemisphere and 'Dionysian' the right.

There is no specific Hindu deity who can be regarded as being guided by the left or the right hemisphere of the brain. However, some symbolic interpretations suggest a connection between the human brain's structure and aspects of Lord Shiva's divine form.

For instance, the 'ventricles' of the human brain are sometimes likened to Lord Shiva's 'trident' (*trishul*) and the 'hypothalamus', to the crescent moon on his head. The brain ventricles are said to maintain internal balance similar to how Lord Shiva maintains the balance in the whole cosmos. The 'hypothalamus' which regulates body's rhythms and emotions, is influenced by the lunar rhythms. The flow of cerebrospinal fluid from the brain to the spine is compared to the sacred river Ganges flowing from Shiva's hair, representing the circulation of vital fluids that support the mind and the body.

Therefore, while no Hindu deity is said to be guided by any of our brain's hemispheres, there are symbolic frameworks that connect the physical brain to divine concepts, particularly in the symbolism of Shiva.

Lord Jesus Worked Through Teresa

Mother Teresa (1910–1997) was born Agnes Gonxha Bojaxhiu in Uskup, Ottoman Empire (now Skopje, North Macedonia) on August 26, 1910. Her family was of Albanian descent. At the age of 12 years, she felt a deep connection to God during a pilgrimage with her mother to the sanctuary at Lourdes in South-Western France. This is the holy place where the Virgin Mary reportedly appeared to a young girl named Bernadette Soubirous in 1858. The Sanctuary of Our Lady of Lourdes is a complex of shrines and religious buildings. Millions of people visit Lourdes annually, drawn to the sacred spring at Massabielle Grotto for taking bath and drinking the water which is known to have healing properties.

This experience confirmed her desire to dedicate her life to serving others as a missionary. In 1928, she joined the Sisters of Loreto. After training and working as a teacher for nearly two decades, she received a direct communication from Jesus. At the age of 36 in 1946, while travelling on a train to Darjeeling, she heard Jesus's voice speaking to her very clearly directing her to leave the convent and serve the poorest of the poor. Jesus said that, if she failed to carry out this order, it would be a breaking of faith on her part. This experience led her to leave her teaching duties and move into the slums of Calcutta to begin her missionary work among the poorest of the poor.

During a period, 10th September 1946 to 3rd December 1947, Mother Teresa had ongoing communication with Jesus through words and visions. Jesus said to her: "I want Indian nuns, victims of my love, who would be Mary and Martha, who would be so united to me as to radiate my love on souls." She set up her Missionaries of the Charity in Calcutta and got the formal permission from Vatican on 7th October 1950. In her own words, its objective was to care for "the hungry, the naked, the homeless, the crippled, the blind, the lepers, all those people who feel unwanted, unloved, uncared for throughout the society and are shunned by everyone".

Mother Teresa was so united with Jesus that she was able to radiate not her love, but Jesus's love through her, and with a human expression. She used to say: "By blood, I am Albanian. By citizenship, I am an Indian. By faith, I am a Catholic nun. As to my calling, I belong to the world. As to my heart, I belong entirely to the Heart of Jesus".

[Privately, Mother Teresa experienced doubts and struggle in her religious beliefs which lasted nearly 50 years, until the end of her life. Mother Teresa expressed grave doubts about God's existence and pain over her lack of faith:

> "Where is my faith?
> Even deep down there is
> nothing but emptiness and darkness……
> If there be God – please forgive me.
> When I try to raise my thoughts to Heaven, there is such convicting
> emptiness that these very thoughts return like
> sharp knives and hurt my very soul."

To my mind, this happened possibly because her 'Bicameral Mind' was not with her all the time. Lord Jesus would leave her to exercise her own *free will* and do things *consciously*. Under such circumstances, her 'Bicameral Mind' will be off and she would be on her own. This problem would have occurred with Abraham, his sons, Moses, Muhammad, Chaitanya Mahaprabhu and Sri Sri Ramakrishna and other spiritually advanced persons in the past, but since there are no documented evidences, we cannot be sure. Since Mother Teresa's is a most recent case, we can risk some speculation.

If the chamber in your mind meant to be occupied by God is full of other things, then God disappears, so empty that chamber of other things so that it becomes full of God (Meister Eckhert, 13th Century German Mystic)

Body Consciousness Lacks Spirituality

Let me share here some ancient Hindu *Bhakti Yoga* poems and relate them to our brain's left and right hemispheres.

> "The man with a body grows hungry
> The man with a body tells lies.
> Do not tear me....the man with a body.
> Just once
> Take on a body like mine
> And see for yourself, O Ramanatha!"

I have taken here a few lines from a poem by Devara Daasimayya, a mid-11th century poet and vachanakaara in Kannada. The lines imply strong urge for 'consumption' which, neuro-scientifically speaking denotes 'Dopamine Hunger' which prompts him, at times, to be deceptive and tell lies. The poet urges to Lord Shiva – the one whom Lord Rama used to worship, to take the human form and see for Himself whether the poet is right or wrong. Beautiful indeed!! The translator of this Kannada poem is H.S. Shivaprakash.

'Consumption' indicates a 'narrow focus' and 'grabbing' propensity which are attributes of the left hemisphere of our brain which is *short-sighted*.

Another example of such *short-sightedness* is in the following poem:

> "The Dude! Bathed, scrubbed, perfumed, tucking in eats till he bloats stud-size
>
> Battering on each pleasure on earth, a germ of *maya* sits concealed in that bulk.
>
> That pampered carcass believes *maya* to be his friend
>
> But *maya* will chew him down to his entrails."

Maya is certainly a hallucinatory function of the left hemisphere which devours our entire consciousness and removes us from the reality. This poem is by Akho, Akha Bhagat or Akha Rahiyadas Soni, 1591–1651, who was a medieval Gujarati poet who wrote in the tradition of the *Bhakti* movement.

Following is a poem where the right hemisphere of the brain speaks. The right hemisphere has a much 'broader view' and, thus, is realistic and far-sighted.

> "This body that you're fussing over,
> This body that you're dolling up,
> This body that you're wearing to the party,
> This body will end as ash."

The poet here is Lal Ded or Lalleshwari, 1320–1392. She was a Kashmiri Shaiva poet who created the *vakh* or *vac* style of mystic poetry. The translator is Ranjit Hoskote. The ash-smeared body of Lord Shiva, yogi-sannyasis and aghoris is a symbol of the impermanent nature of our body.

I am sharing a little longer verse by Guru Ravidas Ji, the 15th-16th century poet from Varanasi, having a similar tone.

> "The walls are made of water, pillared by air,
> sealed together with the mortar of blood,
> and cell of veins and meat and bones
> a cage to hold this poor bird.

Who cares what is yours or mine?
for we nest in this tree only briefly.
As high as you can build, as low as you can dig,
Your size will never swell the dimensions of a grave,

Those lovely curls, that turban tied so rakishly,
they'll soon be turned to ash.
If you've counted on the beauty of your wife and home
without the name of Ram, you've already lost the game.

And me: even though my birth is mean,
my ancestry by everyone, despised,
I have already trusted in you, King Ram,
says Ravidas, a tanner of hides."

Guru Ravidas Ji or Raidas was a 15th–16th century poet at Varanasi. This poem is translated by John Stratton Hawley and Mark Juergensmeyer.

References

1. Julian Jaynes, *The Origin of Consciousness in the Breakdown of the Bicameral Mind*, Boston, New York: A Mariner Book, Houghton Mifflin, 2000.
2. Iain McGilchrist, 'The Divided Brain' Video Interview by Iain McNay, Conscious tv, 17th April 2014.
3. Iain McGilchrist, *The Master and His Emissary: The Divided Brain and the Making of the Western World*, New Haven and London: Yale University Press, New Expanded Paperback Edition, 2019.
4. "The Master and His Emissary" – *Wikipedia.*
5. "Where did Nietzsche tell the story of the Master and His Emissary" – *Philosophy.*
6. "Apollonian and Dionysian" – *Wikipedia.*
7. "Apollo" – *Wikipedia.*
8. "Dionysus" – *Wikipedia.*
9. Sriram Krishnamurthy on Instagram: "In his groundbreaking research…." (Krishnamurthy talks about Dr Tony Nader's research studies on the *Vedic Science*)
10. Surabhi, "Why Hindu Gods Have Multiple Arms and Heads?" *Vedicfeed* 19th June 2023.

11. Mother Teresa – *Wikipedia*
12. Mother Teresa: Biographical, *The Nobel Prize.*
13. David Van Biema, "Mother Teresa's Crisis of Faith", *TIME*, 23 August 2007.
14. "Meister Eckhert: The Mystic Who Found God Within: Life-Changing Teachings Explained" – Video Presentation on YouTube, *The Podcaster Channel,* August 2025.
15. Ed. Arundhathi Subramaniam *A Book of Bhakti Poetry: Eating God*, Gurgaon, India: Penguin Random House India, 2014.

CHAPTER 5

God Brings Oceanic Feeling

The Oceanic Feeling of Romain Rolland

Within the psychoanalytic theory of Sigmund Freud, one should be able to appreciate how a newborn infant feels immediately after coming out of the closet of the mother's womb. It is the infant's first feeling of 'existence', before its ego (the Little 'I') has been formed. The infant gets a feeling of vastness as it had not been aware of the separation between 'self' and 'everything else'. Coined by the Nobel-Laureate French writer and philosopher Romain Rolland in 1927, the term 'Oceanic Feeling' was presented to Sigmund Freud to describe a universal human religious emotion characterised by feelings of eternity – a sensation of oneness with the universe, where personal boundaries dissolve, creating a feeling of unity – and transcendence with something much larger than oneself – limitless.

He was inspired by the example of Sri Sri Ramakrishna, among other mystics, on whom he had researched out of genuine interest. After child Ramakrishna had his first spiritual ecstasy from his 10th or 11th year on, the trances became common, and by the final years of his life, Ramakrishna's *samadhi* periods occurred almost daily. According to Rolland, this feeling is the source of all the religious energy that permeates in various religious systems, and one may justifiably call oneself religious on the basis of this oceanic feeling alone. In his 1929 book *The Life of Ramakrishna*, Rolland distinguished between the feelings of unity and eternity which Ramakrishna experienced in his mystical states, and Ramakrishna's interpretation of those feelings as visions of the Goddess Kali figure. In my analysis, I would like to keep the two experiences separate from each other. Ramakrishna's feelings of unity and eternity was Rolland's *oceanic feeling* whereas his visions of

Goddess Kali were visual hallucinations of the Saint's *Bicameral Mind.* *(References 1&2)*

Sea Followed by Ocean

Rumi was born in 1207 in present-day Afghanistan. The real name for the 13th century Persian poet, mystic and Islamic theologian was Jalal ud-Din Muhammad Rumi. A pivotal figure in Sufism, he was known for his deep love of humanity and philosophy which focused on the spiritual path and divine.

He was profoundly influenced by his spiritual guide, *Shams* of *Tabriz.* His work emphasizes the importance of *love* as the way to understand God's mysteries. He lived most of his life under the Persian Sultanate of *Rum* (wherefrom possibly his name derives) and died in 1273 AD. Upon his death, his followers and his son founded the *Mevlevi* Order, known as the *Order of the Whirling Dervishes,* famous for the Sufi dance known as the *Sama* ceremony.

The profession of the family for several generations was that of Islamic preachers of a relatively liberal school. Rumi was influenced by one of the most famous mystic Persian poets *Attar* who immediately saw Rumi's spiritual eminence. He saw the father walking ahead of the son, and exclaimed: "*Here comes a sea followed by an ocean*". He gave the boy *Asranama,* a book about the entanglement of the soul in the material world. This meeting had a deep impact on the 18-year old Rumi and later on became the inspiration for his works.

Rumi's meeting with the *dervish Shams-e-Tabrizi* on 15 November 1244 completely changed his life from an accomplished teacher and jurist to an ascetic. Sufi's mysticism places great emphasis on the master-disciple relationship in which the younger disciple studies under an older master. The disciple is groomed to reach *fana,* the highest level of spiritual development in Sufism.

Shams had a 'bicameral mind'. He searched and prayed for somebody young who could endure his company. He heard a voice which had asked him: "What will you give him in return?" *Shams* replied:

"My head!". The voice then said: "The one you seek is Jalal ud Din Rumi".

When one day, after having taught him for months, *Shams* disappeared, Rumi searched for him then he realised: "Why should I seek? I am the same as He. His essence speaks through me."

The following verse will explain what kind of questions used to crop up on Rumi's mind:

"Why was I ever created?
Everyday I meditate upon this, and every night I groan,
Why is my own existence to myself the least known?
Whence I have come, why this coming here?
Where to must I go, when will my home to me be shown?
I am in desperate awe, why was I created?
For this, my creation, whatsoever was the reason?
....
I did not come here on my own accord, nor will I thus leave
He who brought me here, shall return me to my very own."

If you visit Lucknow, the capital of Uttar Pradesh, India, don't forget to visit the landmark 'Rumi Gate'. *(References 3&4)*

The *Saint* Who Came as Light from *Satloka* – the Realm of Truth

Many *rishis* have a 'third eye' so there is a story that Kabir came from the *Satloka* by assuming the body of light, and incarnated on a lotus flower in the 'Lahartara' pond. This was witnessed by *rishi Ashtanand* who himself appeared on a lotus flower in the same pond. A few accounts mention that Kabir, in the form of an infant, was found at Lahartara Lake by a Muslim weaver named Niru and his wife Nima, who raised him as their child. As he grew up, he became one of the many disciples of the Bhakti-poet-saint Swami Ramananda of Varanasi, known for devotional Vaishnavism with a strong bent to Advaita philosophy teaching that God was in every person and in everything. Kabir is also regarded as a believer of the Sufi tradition in Islam. The years of

Kabir's birth and death are uncertain. Some favour 1398–1448, while some others favour 1440–1518.

For his poetry, for reasons unknown, Kabir had borrowed from many *dialects* like: Khadi boli, Braj, Bhojpuri, Marwari and Awadhi. In case he possessed a *bicameral mind,* at different times he was getting inspirations and ideas from different divine souls speaking in different languages, not just from one God or Guru. His poems, composed with simple words, cover various aspects of life and call for a loving devotion for God, as well as mysticism and discipline.

I am sharing one of his poems, translated by Rabindranath Tagore, as an example of its spiritual fervour.

> "Where spring, the lord of seasons reigneth,
> there the unstruck music sounds of itself,
>
> There the streams of light flow in all directions,
> few are the men who can cross to that shore!
>
> There, where millions of Krishnas stand with hands folded,
>
> Where millions of Vishnus bow their heads,
> where millions of Brahmas are reading the Vedas,
>
> Where millions of Shivas are lost in contemplation,
> where millions of Indras dwell in the sky,
>
> Where the demi-gods and the munis are unnumbered,
> where millions of Saraswatis, goddess of music play the vina,
>
> There is my Lord, self-revealed,
> and the scent of sandal and flowers dwells in those deeps."

(Kabir, II.57)

Kabir's poems of wisdom are called *banis* (utterances). These were verbally composed in the 15th century and transmitted *orally* through the 17th century. So, discussion on the authenticity of the poems is ongoing. It seems certain that minor changes would have occurred through the centuries and it is also possible that poems written by others have been attributed to Kabir. Rabindranath Tagore's English translation *Songs of Kabir*, was first published in 1915 and has been a classic reprinted and circulated particularly in the West.

The philosophy of Kabir and other *sants* of the Bhakti movement is the seeking of the Absolute – the *Nirguna Brahma* – that there is no distinction between *Soul* and *God*. It urges man to recognize within himself his true divine nature – unselfish, loving and caring. *(References 5-8)*

Sant Meerabai and Her *Madhura Bhava* Mewar

Meerabai was born into a Rathore Rajput royal family in *Kudki* (modern-day Beawar district of Rajasthan), and spent her childhood in Merta. She had a love marriage with Bhoj Raj, the crown prince of Mewar in 1516. Her husband was wounded in one of the ongoing wars with the Delhi Sultanate in 1518, and he died from battle wounds in 1521. Both her father and father-in-law (Rana Sanga) died a few days after their defeat in the Battle of Khanwa against Babur, the first Mughal Emperor. Vikram Singh became the ruler of Mewar. As the story goes, her in-laws tried to assassinate her multiple times. These attempts included sending Meera a glass of poison and telling her it was nectar, and sending her a basket with a snake instead of flowers. She was not harmed in either case, with the snake miraculously becoming a Krishna idol or a garland of flowers.

According to another story, Meera left Mewar and lived in Dwarka or Vrindavan, where she miraculously disappeared by merging into an idol of Krishna after being poisoned by her brother-in-law in 1547. [The Dark God Krishna devoured her by behaving like a *Black Hole*, just like Chaitanya Mahaprabhu disappeared inside the idol of Lord Jagannath in the Puri temple.]

It is widely acknowledged that Meera dedicated her life to Lord Krishna, composing songs of devotion, and was one of the most-important poet-saints of the Bhakti movement period. One of her most popular compositions remains "Payoji maine Ram Ratan dhan payo" ("I have been given the richness of God's name blessing").

Meera speaks of a personal love-centred relationship with Krishna which is manifestation of her *madhura bhava* towards Him, as would be found from the following poem: *(Reference 9)*

> "My *Dark One* has gone to an alien land.
> He has left me behind, he's never returned,
> he's never sent me a single even word.
>
> So I've stripped off my ornaments,
> jewels, and adornments, and cut my hair from my head.
>
> And put on holy garments, all on his account,
> seeking him in all four directions.
>
> Mira: unless she meets the *Dark One,*
> her God, she doesn't even want to live."

(Poem by Meera Bai, Translated by John Straton Hawley)

Servant of the Sun

The 'Servant of the Sun' Surdas could never enjoy the golden rays of the Sun because he was born blind. Everything was *dark* for him. Is that the reason why he had his umbilical cord attached permanently to the Dark God Krishna? A most relevant question!

Surdas was born into a Brahmin family of Uttar Pradesh in 1258. He is celebrated as the pinnacle of poetic artistry in *Braj bhasha* – a language linked to the *Braj* region where Krishna is said to have spent his childhood. His work raised the status of the *Braj Bhasha* from a crude dialect to that of a literary one as the prevalent literary languages were *Persian* or *Sanskrit* in those days.

Surdas was an initiated disciple of Vallabha, the proponent of Pustimarga and his poems formed a central part of Pustimarga liturgical singing-worship. The *Sur Sagar* (Sur's Ocean), which is attributed mainly to Surdas, focuses on descriptions of Krishna as the lovely child of Gokul and Vraj, written from the *gopis'* perspective.

One of his most popular bhajans is: 'Main Naahin Maakhan Khaayo' set to Raga Ramkali. It epitomizes *Vatsalya* (parental love) *Rasa* describing an episode from the *leelas* of Krishna. In the song, Lord Krishna says to his mother that he did not steal the butter, when he was caught by his mother Yashoda with some butter still on his face. He claims: *(References 10&11)*

O Mother of mine, believe me. I have not eaten the butter.

These friends of mine, out of sheer spite, spread some butter on my face.

From a Mute Boy to The Monarch of Hindustani Music

Ramtanu Pandey (1493–1589), who became Mian Tansen later on, was born into a Hindu Brahmin family in Gwalior. His father Mukund Ram was a wealthy poet and musician of Gwalior.

According to some story, Tansen was born mute and did not utter a single word until the age of 5. Was it because his father, who was a priest in Varanasi, had prayed profusely to Kashi Viswanath that the mute boy started speaking and became a legend in the domain of Hindustani Classical Music? Nobody knows. Some say, that a Muslim *Fakir* had met young Ramtanu in the field as a cowherd boy and whispered into his ears and the boy started speaking. But which one is to be believed. Hope the mystery will be revealed some day.

He got his first lessons in Hindustani Classical Music in Madhya Pradesh and got his first break as a musician and composer in the court of Raja Man Singh Tomar of Gwalior and spent most of his adult life in the court and patronage of the Hindu king of Rewa, Raja Ramchandra Singh Baghel where his musical abilities and studies gained widespread fame.

One thing is to be noted here. In those days, a musician used to get appointment in a royal court not only for his vocal or instrumental performance skill but also for his intelligence and talent to compose new Ragas and musical scores. Today, barring a very few rare exceptions most classical musicians get assignments for singing or playing the same Ragas and Raginis again and again. Ability to compose is a very rare talent now-a-days, in the classical music domain.

His fame had attracted the attention of the Mughal Emperor Akbar who requested him to join his court in 1562 at the age of 60. Akbar, being overwhelmed by Ramtanu's musical talent, considered him as one of the *Navaratnas* (nine jewels) in his court and conferred the title of 'Mian' (meaning 'learned man') on him. Mian Tansen was a great composer musician and vocalist as well as an instrumentalist. He had popularized and improved the design of many instruments. Numerous North Indian musical *gharanas* consider him to be their lineage founder.

He is remembered also for his epic *Dhrupad* compositions, creating several new *Ragas*, as well as for writing two classic books on music. According to Hindu legends, for *Dhrupads,* the *bhakti saint* Swami Haridas was the major influence on Tansen. In Islamic biographies, the *Sufi Muslim mystic* Md Ghaus Gwaliori had influenced him. However, evidence suggests that Tansen was less affiliated with either religion, more with music. The presence of musicians like Tansen in Akbar's court was an attempt to accept and integrate the Hindu and Muslim traditions within the Mughal Empire. One legend states that Tansen, apart from his wife Hussaini from Gwalior, had also been married to a daughter of Akbar, named Mehrunissa, for which he had to convert to Islam.

Among the legends about are stories of his bringing down the rains with Raga *Megh Malhar* and lighting lamps by performing Raga *Deepak.* Other legends tell of his ability to bring wild animals to listen with attention (or to talk their language). Once a wild white elephant was captured, but it was fierce and could not be tamed. Finally, Tansen sang to the elephant who calmed down and the emperor Akbar was able to ride on him.

A crater on the planet *Mercury* has been named in Tansen's honour. *(Reference 12)*

The Father of *Qawwali* and the Inventor of *Sitar*: Amir Khusro

Amir Khusro (1253–1325) was an Indo-Persian Sufi singer, musician, composer, poet and scholar, who lived during the period of the Delhi Sultanate. His father was a man of Turkic extraction and mother a native Indian. They were originally settled in what is now known as Uzbekistan; but when it was destroyed by Genghis Khan, they took refuge in the Delhi Sultanate.

Khusro was a very intelligent child. He started learning and writing poetry at the age of nine only. Bugra Khan, the second son of the reigning Sultan became an admirer of Khusro's poetry when he was at his peak of poetic creativity during his twenties. When Bugra Khan was appointed the ruler of Bengal, Khusro visited him. When the Sultan's eldest son Khan Mohammad came to know about him, he invited him to Delhi and then took him to Multan which was the gateway to India for scholars, tradesmen and emissaries from Baghdad, Persia and Arabia to pass through on their way to Delhi.

He was a mystic and a spiritual disciple of Nizamuddin Auliya of Delhi, India. He is regarded as the father of *Qawwali* – (a devotional form of singing of the Sufis). It is a well-punctuated chorus emphasizing the theme and devotional refrain coupled with a lead singer utilising an ornate style of fast *taans* and difficult *svara* combinations are its distinguishing features. *Tarana* and *Trivat* are also credited to Khusro. He is also credited for the invention of the *sitar*, which is a highly modified version of the *Veena*.

Khusro also introduced the *ghazal* style of song in India, both of which still exist widely in India and Pakistan. Khusro's *ghazals* were set to music and were sung by singing girls every night before the Sultan of Delhi. *(Reference 13)*

Liturgical Music

Liturgical music, also known as 'church music' is music composed and performed for use in public worship and religious ceremonies. It serves to *glorify* God (just like the Hindu *mantras* used for worshipping gods and goddesses), foster a deeper 'bonded' connection with the *divine*. It also allows participation within the community, and lift the spiritual experience. Such music originated from the Jewish synagogues, and evolved through periods such as the Gregorian chant and Renaissance. It encompasses various styles like hymns, chants, psalms and polyphonic works, all designed to enhance sacred rites and uphold biblical texts.

Gregorian chant, a popular form, sung in 'monophonic' style is highly suited for worship and dates back to the Middle Ages (9th and 10th centuries). Although popular legend credits Pope Gergory I with inventing Gregorian chant, scholars believe that he only ordered a compilation of melodies throughout the whole Christian world. Traditionally sung by choirs, it is the music of the Roman Rite, performed in the Mass and the monastic Office. It became the official music of the Christian liturgy. Chant was learned in an oral tradition in which the texts and melodies were sung from memory, so notations were not necessary. *(References 14&15)*

Spiritual Music in Islam

Spiritual music in Islam primarily exists within the Sufi tradition, which uses music and chanting for spiritual purposes, such as *Qawwali* and *Dhikr* (remembrance of God). The acceptability of music in Islam varies, with some authorities deeming it forbidden and others, like the Sufi tradition, and theologian *al-Ghazali*, finding it acceptable for spiritual development when it purifies the heart.

Nasheed is also a kind of devotional vocal music in Islam that may or may not involve percussion. Such music can be performed for relaxation, meditation, and spiritual connection. Music's spiritual value depends on the intentions and soul quality of the musician as well as the listener. That simply means, with reference to the Hindu Bharata Muni's *Nava Rasa* theory, you can take only *Bhakti Rasa* as the base of Islamic spiritual music. *(References 16-18)*

References

1. "Oceanic Feeling" – *Wikipedia.*
2. Michael W. Taft, "Non-duality, Freud, and the Oceanic Feeling", *Deconstructing Yourself,* 11th October 2018.
3. "Rumi" – *Wikipedia.*
4. "Rumi/Biography, Poems & Facts" – *Britannica.*
5. "Kabir" – *Wikipedia.*
6. "Kabir" – *Encyclopaedia Britannica.*
7. *One hundred poems of Kabir* (Translated by Rabindranath Tagore), Evelyn Underhill, University of Toronto, 1915.
8. *Songs of Kabir*, (Translated by Rabindranath Tagore), via Gutenberg, 2004.
9. "Mirabai" – *Wikipedia.*
10. "Surdas" – *Wikipedia.*
11. "Main Naahin Maakhan Khaayo" – *Wikipedia.*
12. "Tansen" – Wikipedia.
13. "Amir Khusrau" – *Wikipedia.*
14. "Liturgical Music" – *Wikipedia.*
15. "Gregorian chant" – *Wikipedia.*
16. "Spiritual Music in Islam" – *Wikipedia.*
17. "Nasheed" – *Wikipedia.*
18. "Navarasa" – *Wikipedia.*

CHAPTER 6

Human Mind: Consciousness

Our Mind of All Seasons

The human mind is a marvellous creation of nature. It has nature's all seasons in it. It has summer, monsoon, autumn, winter, and spring. It has heat, drought, cold, snowfall, rains, thunder, storm, and flood. However, your marvellous mind becomes your kingdom only when it is totally under your control. That happens under the following circumstances: (i) when you are in 'nirvikalpa samadhi' – you are in thoughtless 'trance'; (ii) when you are in 'savikalpa samadhi' – you are in a 'Flow Brain State' ('FBS'); (iii) your mind is engaged in a meaningful task – your brain's 'Task Mode Network' ('TMN') circuit is on. All such circumstances take place only when your mind is *conscious*. During sleep, day-dreaming, your mind is not under your control. It lacks *consciousness*. It also lacks *consciousness* when you are engaged in some routine tasks and your task performance is automatic. *Consciousness* is only a small part of our mental life as unconscious thoughts and ideas, unconscious judgments make up the majority of our mental processes.

When faced with a non-routine situation, sitting down and thinking out what to do is a sign of *conscious mind*. And the *conscious mind* will think in terms of *metaphors*, such as 'it is a hard problem' or 'I can handle it with difficulty'. The *conscious mind* introspects.

Can our mind remain vacant – unless we make it vacant by going into *nirvikalpa samadhi*? Vacant mind is devil's workshop, and the devil is our 'Default Mode Network' ('DMN') circuit which gets automatically switched on when we are not engaged in any task. Do we see *visions* or *hear voices* when the mind is otherwise unoccupied to earn the easily available neuro-transmitter *Dopamine* because unless you have practised and developed the habit of *Dopamine Fasting* ('DF'), the brain needs to have *Dopamine* released from its 'Reward Circuit' from time to time by any means. Schizophrenics and other psychotic patients hallucinate when there is an overdose of *Dopamine* in the brain.

Location of Consciousness

Consciousness – if it is thought as a thing, then like all other things, it must have a location, and the obvious answer is: it is located inside the head. This is because, when we introspect, we sometimes even close our eyes to look inward on an inner space sometimes behind the eyes. Moreover, we seem to look at different directions. We also assume that there is a space for consciousness in others' heads too. In talking to another person, we maintain periodic eye-to-eye contact assuming a space for consciousness in others' heads too, similar to the space we imagine inside our own heads where we are talking from.

In yogic sciences, there is a very important *nerve plexus*, the *ajna chakra*, located in between the two eyebrows, where biologically the 'Pineal Gland' ('PG') is located. The 'PG' is known as the *Third Eye* which is said to connect people to their intuition, give them the ability to communicate with the world, or help them receive messages from the past and the future.

The philosopher and scientist who proposed that the 'PG' is the location of the soul was the 17th century Frenchman Rene Descartes (1596–1650). He theorized that the gland was the principal seat of the soul because it was the only midline structure in the brain that was singular and capable of movement, making it a suitable interface for the connection between the mind and the body. Descartes had thought that 'PG' was the centre for *rational consciousness*.

The *reticular formation* is a complex, net-like network of neurons and nuclei in the brainstem that serves as a crucial integration and relay centre for brain functions, regulating *consciousness*, sleep, attention, and autonomic functions like respiration and blood pressure. It receives sensory input and projects throughout the nervous system, enabling the modulation of motor activities, filtering sensory stimuli and maintaining wakefulness. *Reticular formation* is the place where general anaesthesia produces its effect by deactivating the neurons. Cutting it produces permanent sleep and coma. Stimulating it through an implanted electrode in most of its regions wakes up a sleeping animal. Moreover, it is capable of grading the activity of most other parts of the brain. *(References 1-3)*

Consciousness Led to the Fall of Man

God is good, kind, benevolent and loving. He gives you freedom to exercise your will, but does not like when you transgress the limits. Lucifer was cast from Heaven for his ego-driven rebellion. He is traditionally identified with the Satan or the Devil, the adversary of God and ruler of Hell.

The story of Milton's *Paradise Lost* is based on two narratives, one about Satan (Lucifer) and the other about Adam and Eve. It begins after Satan and the other fallen angels had been defeated and banished to Hell, or, as it is called in the poem, Tartarus. Satan volunteered to corrupt the newly created Earth and God's new and most favoured creation – the mankind, which was endowed with *consciousness* – free will and volition. (In fact, that was the mistake God had made as he had lost sight of the fact that the first humans created had absolutely no foresight; and this weakness of the first humans was taken advantage of by the cunning Satan.).

Satan entered God's new **material world**, which was full of temptations for a-spiritual enjoyment (for earning the easily earnable neurotransmitter *Dopamine*, if you allow me to look at the situation from the viewpoint of neuroscience). He went straight to the Garden of Eden where God had created world's first human couple – Adam and Eve.

God had given Adam and Eve total freedom and mastery over all creation, but he had given them one explicit command: not to eat from the tree of the knowledge of good and evil, lest they would face the penalty of death. That was the limit God had set for them. World's first human couple had a heart-to-heart romantic relationship and thus remained without sin. Satan disguised in the form of a serpent, could successfully tempt Eve to pluck a fruit from the forbidden tree and eat it. Adam soon followed Eve and committed the same sin. He declared to Eve that since she was made from his flesh, they are bound to each other – if she died, he must also die.

After eating the fruit, Adam and Eve experienced physical attraction and lust for the first time; and it rendered their sexual encounter with one another unpleasant. They soon fell asleep and had terrible nightmares, and after they woke up, they experienced guilt and shame for the first time.

Meanwhile, Satan returned triumphantly to Hell. He told his fallen fellow angels about how their scheme had worked and Mankind had fallen, giving them complete dominion over Paradise. As he finished his speech, however, the fallen angels around him became hideous snakes, and soon enough, Satan himself turned into a snake, deprived of limbs and unable to talk. Thus, they shared the same punishment, as they shared the same guilt.

Eve now appealed to Adam for reconciliation of their actions. They approached God seeking forgiveness. Archangel Michael showed Adam a vision where he witnessed everything that would happen to mankind until the Great Flood. Michael told him about Mankind's potential redemption from original sin through Jesus Christ (who Michael addressed as the 'King Messiah'). Adam and Eve were cast out of Eden, and Michael said that Adam might find a *paradise* within himself. Adam and Eve now had a more distant relationship with God, who is omnipresent but invisible.

And, Michael's prediction came true. God gave Adam and Eve *bicameral minds* without any *consciousness*. They possessed the potential to hear voices from God through the right side of their brains (the 'input provider') to cope with new and novel situations and solve practical problems while they could handle their day-to-day living and working with the help of the left side of their brains (the 'output producer'). *(Reference 4)*

Subjective Conscious Mind

The word *psyche* encompasses both conscious and unconscious mental processes, The *conscious mind* is a part of the *psyche* focused on immediate awareness and rational thought.

From another angle, *conscious* mind is just the tip of the 'iceberg' which represents the whole mind. Below this tip of *consciousness*, the bulk of our mental activities take place in the 'semi-conscious', 'subconscious' and 'unconscious' realms.

Subjective conscious mind is an *analog*, or direct representation, of what is called the 'real world'. It is built up with a vocabulary or lexical field whose terms are all *metaphors* or *analogs* of activities in the physical world. It is intimately bound up with volition and decision. We mostly use 'visual' terms to describe conscious processes: brilliant, bright, clear, dull, obscure – these are all 'visual' *metaphors*. The *metaphors* that we use to describe physical behaviour are: quick, slow, agitated, strong, weak. The *metaphor* helps to generate *consciousness*; it helps you to be *conscious* rather than if you simply describe something. *Consciousness* is thus the work of lexical *metaphors*.

It came after the development of language. If that be so, then it is of much more recent origin than has heretofore supposed. The first human writings in hieroglyphics, hieratic, and cuneiform – all began about 3,000 BC, Therefore, whether *consciousness* was present in the early Egyptian dynasties and in Mesopotamian culture are thus too ambiguous.

When written script had not been discovered, in oral communication, one used to get accustomed to in one's own mother tongue – he could not follow any other language spoken by another person from a different tribe, community, or culture. Under such circumstances, activities to which one was habituated as those would be performed regularly effortlessly, the performer did not need to be *conscious*.

Consciousness and Learning & Thinking

Consciousness is not necessary for any learning. As a matter of fact, learning takes place unconsciously. Consciousness takes you into the task, giving you the goal to be reached. But from thereon, learning is unconscious. In fact, consciousness can be quite undesirable. Consciousness is also not necessary for thinking – logical, rational or creative, beyond setting a goal.

The Gods

Who then were the gods that pushed men about like robots and sang epics through their lips? They were *voices* whose speech and directions could be as distinctly heard by the Iliadic heroes as voices can be heard by certain epileptic and schizophrenic patients or just as Joan of Arc heard her voices. The gods were organisations of the central nervous system. The gods are what we now call hallucinations. Usually they are only seen and heard by the particular hearer they are speaking to. The strongest emotion which the hero felt toward a god is amazement or wonder, the kind of emotion that we feel when the solution of a particularly difficult problem suddenly pops into our heads, or in the cry of *eureka!* from Archimedes in his bath.

Let me compare the human mind with a geographical terrain. Is it mountainous (peaks and valleys)? Or, is it hilly (ups-and-downs)? Or, is it plain (no turbulence, absolutely at peace)? Or, is it oceanic (a feeling of oneness with the universe or God)? Or, is it a place where you have visions and hear voices originating from nowhere? What is 'Conscious Mind'?

French philosopher Rene Descartes (1596–1650) linked *consciousness* to the undeniable act of 'thinking', famously asserting "I think, therefore I am" (*cognito ergo sum*). He defined 'thought' broadly to include any self-aware mental activity, believing 'consciousness' to be an indubitable mental phenomenon distinct from the physical body. This concept, *Cartesian dualism*, established 'consciousness' as the essence of the 'self'.

Goddesses: Equally Superior

The ancient world was matriarchal. At the dawn of civilisation, man's concept of divinity was localised in the softer gender – in femininity, because of its motherly role. Husbands and fathers were non-entities. In India, the wedlock system was introduced by the great sage Svetketu, according to the narratives in the epic *Mahabharata*. The matriarchal trend prevailed in Egypt, Greece, Mesopotamia, as well as in the Indus Valley (Mohenjodaro and Harrappa) – in the profile and personality of Virgin Mary. To my mind, she symbolised the fact that father was an absentee entity – that a progeny could be created and brought up singly by the mother. Modern brain science also confirms that a child inherits its forebrain (cerebral cortex) features such as intelligence, imagination and creativity from the mother and the midbrain (limbic system etc.) features such as emotions and partnership drives from the father. It is therefore natural for the mother to claim the ownership of her children.

What does one mean by the feminine power? Feminine power is hidden in her unconditional love and affection, her motherliness, her sacrifice, and her relentless service before self. Mother Mary has little Jesus clinging to her on her lap, the wounded soldier in the battlefield crying for her mother before his life force is extinguished, the young patient waking up from his coma in the hospital, post- surgery, is searching for his mother. Mother is the much sought-after Goddess, no inferior to a God.

In ancient India, there were female sages also who were conversant with mantras, stotras, and shastras. In the domain of spirituality, men and women had equal rights. In the household, the lady of the house was in charge.

Sri Sri Ma Sarada Devi saw Thakur Ramakrishna everywhere. Once she prevented one of her attendants from hurting an ant as she saw Ramakrishna in the tiny creature. She used to reside inside a divine bubble – very personal and private. She had held on to him with strong, firm hands. His silent wisdom had helped her to start a quiet revolution to discover the truth, the authentic reality.

The Eating God

The Hindu God Lord Jagannath of Puri, Odisha, India is known as the 'Eating God' or *Bhog Khaiya* (one who eats a lot of food offered to Him) due to the large quantities of food offerings (*bhog*) that are daily presented to him. These offerings, including the famous *Chappan Bhog* (56 different dishes), are considered highly auspicious and reflect the devotion of his followers. A myth suggests that after Lord Krishna did not eat or drink to protect Braj from Indradev, her mother Yashoda and the people of Braj offered him 56 dishes in an act of love. This practice was then extended to other forms of Lord Vishnu, including Jagannath. In a legend from the Laxmi Purana, it's stated that if the household deity, Lakshmi, is displeased, the brothers (Jagannath and Balabhadra) will have nothing to eat, showing the importance of food in their divine lives.

Whether Lord Jagannath exists or not, the practice is symbolic and has a scientific value. Out of the several neuro-chemicals secreted inside our brain to facilitate and modulate different functions, two most important ones are: 'Dopamine' ('D') and 'Serotonin' ('S'). 'D' is the most common 'feel good' chemical which is secreted when we feel happy. 50 percent of 'D' is released from the 'Reward Circuit' of the upper cranial brain that we have located between our two ears. And, the balance 50 percent is secreted in the 'gut' brain in our digestive system when we enjoy our food. And, as regards 'S' which is responsible for keeping us in 'good mood', only 5 to 10 percent is secreted in the head brain and the bulk 90 to 95 percent is released in the gut brain and is linked with consumption of food. Thus, consumption of healthy and balanced diet is essential for our physical and mental health. This is the lesson one must take from the 'Eating God' of Hinduism.

While people, in general, will take such a lesson from this 'Eating God' example, I will share a different point of view. How can a God who has no hands and feet consume 56 items of food served to him? Is it thus symbolic to tell the devotees that you may be surrounded by many attractive items for consumption but restrain yourselves. Let your brain cells not release the excitatory brain chemical *glutamate*; instead let it tap the source of the inhibitory neurotransmitter *GABA*.

God: With Form Or Formless

God exists with a form (*sakar*) and also without a form (*nirakar*). He is present with all his qualities, perceptible to the devotee (*saguna*) and without his qualities and attributes perceptible from outside (*nirguna*). It is easy to be *conscious* about God in his full form; which is not the case when he is formless but his voice can be heard. That was the case in the *bicameral era*.

In the epic *Mahabharata*, Arjuna had asked Lord Krishna: who was his preferred devotee – one who worshipped him in his full form or another who was devoted to his formless existence. In terms of modern cosmology and astrophysics, these respectively correspond to: 'Dark Matter' ('Krishna Bastu') and 'Dark Energy' ('Krishna Shakti'). In his response, God said that both were equally devoted to him and thus preferred equally, but there was one marked difference. The Lord was easy to be worshipped in his physical form as he could be experienced sensorily; whereas his formless existence was difficult to comprehend – devotees had to work harder to experience him as formless although being formless he was all-pervading, present everywhere like 'Dark Energy' is passing through our bodies all the time although we are totally unaware. The Lord said that since we have a physical body, it is easy to appreciate God in his physical form with all his attributes (*'saguna'*).

Hands: Vehicle of the Mind; Use of Hands in Worship

Worshipping an idol with one hand is generally acceptable in Hindu practice, as the primary emphasis is on the priest's or devotee's *bhava* or devotional feeling. However, if we look at it from the point of view of neuroscience, we come up with some critical observation regarding using only the right hand. Right hand, in right-handed people, is controlled by the left hemisphere of the brain which lacks the deep devotional oceanic feeling, the source of which is the right hemisphere that controls the left hand. Besides, right hand is the 'grasping' (in other words, 'controlling') hand which we use for 'eating' (in other words, 'consumption') that stimulates the Dopaminergic neural circuits in the 'head' as well as the 'gut' brain. Ideally, a Hindu priest or devotee must make it a point to use the *anjali mudra* (*namaste* gesture) with the palms pressed firmly together, with the fingertips pointing upwards, held near the heart (*anahata chakra*). This gesture generates the deep oceanic feeling and it is a sign of respect, devotion, and humility towards the divine. It also symbolises a complete surrender to God, embodying the belief that by offering everything to the divine, one can receive help and grace. The best practice for a Hindu priest would be to keep both his hands engaged while worshipping – one hand holding a bell and other engaged in an incense pot. Avatar Sri Sri Ramakrishna often used both hands, or his hands interchangeably for worshipping Goddess Kali. In some accounts, he used his right hand to gesture heavenly, asking questions about the nature of the divine, and the left hand in a questioning gesture.

Muslims use both hands in prayer (*Salah*). The exact placement of hands do vary slightly between the different schools of Islamic jurisprudence.

Christians lift their hands during prayer, as:

expression of love and dependence
as a gesture of surrender ('my life is in your hands') and worship
to invite God's presence and power into service openness
as a request for cleansing from every sin.

Metaphor

All thinking, most obviously philosophical and scientific thinking is at the bottom *metaphorical* in nature. Although we are familiar with the *metaphors*, we don't notice their existence in our everyday life. It is the *metaphors* that provide the 'something else'. It is *metaphor* that carry us across the implied gap between dry language and the world.

Metaphor is the use of a term for one thing to describe another because of some kind of similarity between them. There are thus always two terms in a metaphor, the thing to be described – the *metaphrand* and the thing or relation used to elucidate it – the *metaphier*. It is by metaphor that language grows. Indeed, language is an organ of perception, not simply a means of communication; and metaphors do provide a better perception. Metaphors thus give a new shape and form to language, creating new circumstances.

Metaphors can bring unconscious meanings into conscious awareness, allowing for new insights and perspectives. Metaphors provide a framework for understanding abstract concepts by connecting them to concrete familiar ones, thereby building our consciousness of those concepts.

Julian Jaynes argued that *consciousness* itself is an emergent property of metaphorical thinking. He suggested that our ability to model subjective mental experiences as 'things' within a simulated space is what gives rise to the subjective feeling of consciousness.

'Metaphor' is to designate a particular aspect of a thing or to describe something for which specific words are not available. In forming a 'metaphor', we bring concepts from whatever we see in the real world. Is the use of a 'metaphor' helpful in generating 'consciousness' about a thing – to make one understand the thing much better in practical terms? Nouns, pronouns, verbs, adjectives, adverbs, prepositions, conjunctions are not enough to develop complete *consciousness* about something in the mind of the listener or the reader. 'Metaphors' are used to develop complete *consciousness*. '*Consciousness*' can be said as made of 'metaphors'. For example, taste the use of 'metaphors' in the following expressions: "the mountains and hills of my high imagination", and "the plains, and caves and caverns of my memory".

There is, therefore, a similarity between *consciousness* and the physical-behavioural world we are conscious of. We are never 'conscious' of things in their true nature. 'Consciousness' can only have arisen in the human species, and that development must have come after the development of language, in its complete form.

The earliest writings of mankind were on stone, clay, or papyrus so that those could be SEEN, rather than just HEARD. In human history, it happened around 3,000 BC. None of the writings is entirely understood as they were in hieroglyphics, hieratics, or cuneiform. So, whether 'consciousness' was present in early Egyptian dynasties and in Mesopotamian cultures, is thus too ambiguous for the kind of concerned analysis which is required.

Neanderthal people, who had appeared before our species, the *homo sapiens*, had created cave art with their unconscious mind.

If you take Homer's epic *Iliad*, no word for 'free will' or 'volition' can be found. In *Iliad*, gods take the place of *consciousness* (representing 'free will' or 'volition'). The beginnings of actions do not originate from any conscious plans, reasons, or motives – they are the outcomes of instructions or commands from God. Men in those days had no 'ego' either (please refer to Rene Descartes's 'I think therefore, I am' – here 'I' represents the 'ego'). In 'spiritualty', we recommend, shedding of the 'ego' – the 'free will'.

The Myceneans were the first advanced Greek civilised people on the Greek mainland during the Late Bronze Age (1750–1050 BC). Named after their major city, Mycenae, they are often associated with the heroes and legends of Homer's *Iliad* and *Odyssey*. In distinction to our own 'Subjective Conscious Minds', psychologist Julian Jaynes of Princeton University, called the mentality of the Mycenaeans, governed by a *Bicameral Mind* which has no 'consciousness' (that is, volition, planning etc.) and executes tasks as 'told' to the individual in his own familiar rudimentary language without any 'metaphors', sometimes with the *visual aura* of a familiar friend, or authority figure, or 'god' or sometimes by a 'voice' alone. The individual obeyed these hallucinated voices because he could not 'decide' himself – what to do.

According to Damodar Savarkar (1883–1960), the roots of the phenomenon of *Hinduness* ('Hinduttva') can be traced back to the very dawn of unitary human consciousness in this part of the planet. One needs to look at developments that started in the Indo-Iranian region around 2,500 BCE and lasted at least till 700 BCE.

According to Julian Jaynes, from the pre-historic to the end of the ancient urban civilisation – estimated to be around 1,200 BCE, humanity had not successfully integrated the two hemispheres of the brain. The intuitive right hemisphere was the master and the analytical left hemisphere simply executed – subordinate to the intuitive flashes that appeared in the right hemisphere. The right hemisphere intuitions were received as auditory hallucinations which in turn were accepted as the voices of gods. In other words, there was a time in human civilisation when gods (and goddesses) literally 'spoke'. In certain cases, there could be voices of 'devils' or 'demons' that could also be heard.

However, with the emergence of urban civilisation, the *bicameral mind* could not support the increasing complexity and related stress. The development of writing too was a factor in undermining the 'gods' of the *bicameral mind.* Soon a void developed. *Bicameral mind*-based civilisations collapsed or got transformed into civilisations where the individual *SELF* evolved. There was no individual *SELF* in the *bicameral mind.* It was with the breakdown of the *bicameral mind* that *consciousness* emerged.

The Hindu *Vedas* were bicameral. From the *Vedas,* the Hindus of India hurtled into the ultra-subjective *Upanishads.* In the Indian context, the *bicameral mind,* rather than breaking down got integrated into a higher and holistic *SELF* through a systematic cultivation of inner discipline. This is well attested in Harappan iconography as well as in the Vedic literature. *Atharva Veda* hints that all gods abide within man as cows in the cow pen.

As Vedic deities became silent, the concept of *ritual* became symbolic of a cosmic order. During the Vedic days, Gods were a living presence. The worshippers established a sense of deep intimacy, trust and affinity with them. Everything around was astir with divinity, instinct with life. The Fire was no ordinary fire; it was most sacred. The Earth was no ordinary earth – she was the Mother, But this kind of approach is possible only when man is in a state of innocence as it seems he was during the ancient Vedic days. The Vedic Gods suffered deflation in the hands of the Upanishadic sages who taught *brahmavada* and *atmavada.*

Upanishadic *atmavada* was an attempt to recover the old sense of intimacy with Gods but under new conditions when they had withdrawn themselves from before the eyes of man behind a veil. Later on, *Yoga* came. It was an attempt to discover methods and processes by which to enter the depths of the heart where Gods had retired under increasingly more difficult conditions. However, eventually, with the passage of time, instead of the complete breakdown and subduing of the right hemisphere to the left, a flexible harmony became the goal of the Hindu intellectuals. Vedic deities changed and evolved into the main gods and goddesses of Hinduism, retained both the playful intuitive qualities of the *bicameral* phase while integrating themselves with further exploration of other dimensions of the *Inner Self.*

The collapse of the *bicameral mind* was dealt with by the Hindus and by the Iranians in fundamentally different ways. While Hindus opted for one Unity, Iranians opted for one God.

What *Consciousness Is Not*

'Consciousness' is not what we generally think it is. It is not to be confused with 'reactivity' – how we react in a particular situation. We become 'reactive' without being *conscious*. By 'reactive', I mean either 'aggressive' or 'apprehensive and aloof'.

'Consciousness' is not a very powerful lamp that we get in a surgical theatre which illuminates the whole area so that the surgical team has a clear sight. Instead, it is like a torchlight that illuminates only the portion that needs to be focussed – the rest remains dark. 'Focus' is the 'metaphor' that we use when we wish somebody to be *conscious* about a particular thing.

'Consciousness' usually has a role in learning a complex activity like playing the piano or singing vocal classical music, but not necessarily in its performance which becomes 'unconscious'. In fact, consciousness could be quite damaging in the 'performance' stage.

'Consciousness' is not the 'copy paste' of any experience. Conscious experiences cannot be put together to form a concept.

'Consciousness' is not necessary for 'thinking', 'reasoning' or 'making judgments'.

'Consciousness' need not, barring exceptions, be involved in speaking, writing, listening, or reading.

Greatest Insights of Mankind: Mysterious in Origin

The greatest insights of mankind have always been most mysterious in origin.

I am sharing a few examples below.

Carl Friedrich Gauss (1777–1855), the outstanding German mathematician and astronomer, referred to an arithmetical theorem which he had unsuccessfully tried to prove for years, how like a sudden flash of lightning, the riddle happened to be solved. He himself could not figure out what was the thread that connected what he previously knew with what made his present success possible.

Herman von Helmholtz (1821–1894), the German physicist and physician had his happy thoughts which often enough crept quietly into his thinking without his recognizing their vital importance. In a few other cases, they arrived suddenly, without any *conscious* effort on his part.......they liked especially to make their appearance while he was taking a stroll over crowded hills in sunny weather.

Friedrich August Kekule (1829–1896), the famous German organic chemist claimed that he had a daydream or dream of a snake seizing its own tail which did inspire him to discover the ring structure of *benzene*. This vision provided the crucial insight that benzene's six carbon atoms were arranged in a circular, or hexagonal pattern, a discovery that revolutionised organic chemistry and led to the development of aromatic compounds. The dream that suggested that the six carbon atoms in *benzene* were connected in a ring – a concept previously unimagined by chemists.

Dmitri Mendelev (1834–1907), the great Russian chemist had saw in a dream a table where all elements fell into place as required. As he woke up, he immediately wrote it down on a piece of paper, only in one place did a correction later seem necessary.

Henri Poincare (1854–1912), the brilliant French mathematician described how he set out on a geologic excursion and the incidents on the journey made him forget his mathematical work. Having reached the commune of Coutances in Normandy, France, they entered an omnibus to go some place or other. At the very moment when he put his foot on the step, without anything in his former thoughts seeming to have paved the way for it, the transformation he had used to define the Fuchsian functions were identified with those of non-Euclidian geometry.

The Danish physicist Niels Bohr (1885–1962) had witnessed a dream where he saw the electrons of an atom orbiting the nucleus in a manner similar to planets orbiting the sun. This vision, which he described as inspirational, provided the key insight for the revolutionary atomic model, for which he was awarded the Nobel Prize in Physics in 1922.

James Watson and Francis Crick, discovered DNA's Double-Helix Structure, built upon the work of Rosalind Franklin in England.

A Race without Consciousness

If the above is correct, then it is perfectly possible that there could have existed a race of men who spoke, judged, reasoned, solved problems, indeed did most of the things for their daily living and working, but were not *conscious* at all. There was a civilisation without any *consciousness* whatsoever.

Moreover, there still are a few rare individuals, totally extraordinary, who get sudden flashes of insights and revelations which form the bases of their discoveries in science or miraculous creative thoughts that enrich the domains of art, literature, music, dance, and dramatics. See one such example from the man who has revolutionised the domain of physical sciences, Albert Einstein (1879–1955).

> A close friend of Einstein's once said to a co-faculty
> that many of the physicist's greatest ideas came to
> him so suddenly while he was shaving that he had to
> move the blade of the razor very carefully each morning,
> lest he cut himself with surprise.

And a well-known physicist in Britain once told another famous physicist – "We often talk about the three B's - the Bus, the Bath, and the Bed. That is where the great discoveries are made in our science". *(References 5-8)*

References

1. "Ajna" – *Wikipedia.*
2. 'Descartes, the pineal soul, and brain stem death' – *Britannica.*
3. 'Reticular Formation' – *Wikipedia.*
4. "Paradise Lost" – *Wikipedia.*
5. Edited by Swami Prabhananda, *Sarada-Anudhyan*, Kolkata: Ramakrishna Mission Institute of Culture, 4th Impression, July 2020.
6. Julian Jaynes, *The Origin of Consciousness in the Breakdown of the Bicameral Mind*, Boston, New York: A Mariner book (Houghton Mifflin Company), 2000.
7. Iain McGilchrist, *The Master and His Emissary: The Divided Brain and the Making of the Western World*, New Haven & London: Yale University Press, 2009.
8. Aravindan Neelakandan, "Gods, God, Unity, Unit", *Swarajya,* 11th March 2015; Updated 11th February 2016.

CHAPTER 7

Human Nature

Bicamerality

Human nature is split into two distinctly different chambers. Thus, it can be described as *bicameral.* These two chambers are: an 'input-provider' part and an 'output-producer' part, which could be in so many different combinations: parent-child; teacher/tutor/professor/ instructor/class notes/text books/published bazar notes – student; trainer- participant; lecturer- attendee; guru-disciple; boss-subordinate; master-servant; employer-employee; counsellor-counselee; mentor-mentee; husband-wife and vice versa; books/journals/internet- scholar-researcher. The 'input-provider' provides 'inputs' in the form of lessons, instructions, tips, advices, counsel and so on, and the output-producer follows meticulously and translates those into practice without any original contribution at all. The 'output-producer' is thus totally dependent on the 'input-provider'. Only, in exceptional cases, where the 'output-producer' has improved upon the quality and content of the 'inputs' received, he (no gender bias) is different from the common geese. He has the 'swan' like mind. And, if he can bring about a '180 to 360' degree acceptable change to the 'input' received, then I would describe him as a 'black swan'. 'Durga Idol' is the basic 'input'. Now, if the image-maker brings about a '180 to 360' degree appreciable change in the form, then he is a 'white swan' (180 degree) or a 'black swan' (360 degree). The blind 'repeater/copier' has no 'free will' as he is copying it in verbatim totally 'unconsciously'. The 'improviser/ improver' has a 'free will' and he is using it 'consciously'

There was a time in the history of mankind, when there were no organised 'groups' with proper 'leaders' ('tribes' existed without any acceptable leadership) common man was not 'conscious' – he was entirely dependent on instructions and commands received from the 'input-provider' part of his bicameral mind – which he regarded as the voice of God or His messenger, an Angel. He used to follow those literally, without any amendment *per se*. Even when families were formed, in joint families, there would be a 'head of the family' who had to be consulted in every case of decision-making or problem-solving. The 'joint family' culture gave way to the 'nuclear family' concept. Even there was a 'head of the family'. But, even, that culture is giving way to the 'individual' orientation where each family member is guided by his own 'ego' and, the family is a battlefield of 'egos' instead of being a happy, peaceful organisational unit.

Eric Berne's Ego-states

Let us look at the situation using Dr Eric Berne's 'Ego-state' concept.

Eric Berne, MD (1910–1970) was a Canadian-born psychiatrist. He was a very keen observer of human behaviour not as a researcher in any university. He was engaged in chamber practice and had the good habit of maintaining patient records, including for their follow-up sessions, meticulously. Afterwards, he used to go through those with a keen observer's mind and tried to find some specific trends as to how people behaved. *(References 1&2)*

To summarise his findings, when a child is born, it is simple, innocent, absolutely ego-less. So that is what he described as the 'Child' (C) ego-state. An 'Obedient Child' (OC) accepts the parents as 'input-provider' and obeys the parental orders, instructions, commands blindly as 'output-producer'. The OC has no 'consciousness' or 'free will'. The relationship is 'super' – there is no conflict; everything happens absolutely smoothly, without any hassle. Such smooth transactions would take place between the two spouses and a parent and a child or in two siblings, between two friends, or in a boss-subordinate or employer-employee, master-servant relationship if the 'ego-states' of both are not in conflict, instead quite compatible with each other.

Now, meanwhile, the Child is growing and it uses its brain's *mirror neurons* to copy the behaviour of its Parent. 'Parents' are also of two types, Berne had observed. The first kind is 'Critical Parent' (CP) who is highly autocratic, most egoistic and demanding, has high expectations from the (C). The other kind is just the opposite in nature – most kind, benevolent and considerate, nourishing and nurturing (NP). If the child is born with a sober soul, it will copy the (NP) and with its peers may behave as (NP) while transacting with them behaviourally. However, on the contrary, if it is born with a rebellious streak in its soul, it will copy the (CP) and its own 'Child' ego-state would be argumentative, disobedient, breaking peace and harmony being defiant – decribed in one word as the 'Rebellious Child' (RC). There is no problem with an (OC) – all problems arise while handling an (RC). The (RC) does not always accept the (P) as the 'input-provider' and, therefore, does not function properly as an 'output-producer'.

[An example of 'Bicameral Mind' is that of a 'Rastafarian' who is a follower of the 'Rastafari' movement, a religion and social movement that originated in Jamaica in the 1930s, centered on the belief that Ras Tafari Makonnen, later Emperor Haile Selassie I of Ethiopia, is a divine figure (Jah) and returned Jesus Christ. *(Reference 3)*

Read the lyrics of a Rastafarian' song which indicates that a true Rastafarian is totally dependent on 'Jah' and lacks 'consciousness' and 'free will'.

> "Hail Jah Ta Fari....Hail Jah Ta Fari
> Hail Him for Everything
> Hail Him for Food
> Hail Him
> Hail Him for Shelter
> Hail Him
> Hail Him for Clothes
> Hail Him.......Hail Him for Everything.
> Hail Jah Ta Fari........Hail Jah Ta Fari
> Hail Him Before You Go to Your Rest
> Hail Him......Hail Him
> Hail Him When You Wake Up and See the Light
> Hail Him ....Hail Him

Hail Him Without an Apology……Hail Him
Hail Him Imperial Majesty
Hail Jah Ta Fari …….Hail Jah Ta Fari
Jah Ta Fari
Hail Him for Guidance
Hail Him for Protection
Hail Him for Providence
Hail Him for Everything, Everything Which Is Good
Hail Jah Ta Fari…….Hail Jah Ta Fari…….Hail Jah
And I and I Don't in League with Anything Wrong
And I and I Speak About Right
So I and I Would Have to Hail Him
Hail Jah Ta Fari ……..Hail Jah Ta Fari
Hail Him for Everything Which Is Good
Hail Him Without an Apology ……Hail Him
Hail Jah Ta Fari……..Hail Jah Ta Fari."

(*Source:* 'Burning Spear- 'Hail' Heat Wave')

Here, the Rastafarian is behaving like an 'Obedient Child' (OC) to the 'divine soul' 'Jah' whom he regards as a 'Nurturing Parent' (NP)]

When two individuals are transacting or interacting with each other from the (Parent) (P) plane, there is no problem because they have identical (P) 'ego-states'. Same is the case when it is a (Child) (C) to (Child) (C) transaction.

I, being a Brain Science scholar, have related Eric Berne's 'Transactional Analysis' (TA) principle to the 'Brain Theory' and also to Julian Jaynes's *Bicameral Mind* theory. Berne's (Parents) are the 'input-providers' and thus in the 'Right Brain' (RB) and his (Child) the 'output-producer' is in the 'Left Brain' (LB) which has neither any 'consciousness', nor any 'free will'.

When the (C) grows and develops 'consciousness' and 'free will', his 'Adult' (A) 'ego-state' develops. And an (A) can be understood, appreciated and be compatible with another (A) who is 'conscious' and has 'free will'. An (A) therefore, is not compatible with a (P) or a (C).

This is how Berne's 'TA' takes a new form after I've looked at it from (i) the human brain theory, and (ii) the 'bicameral mind' concept.

In the *bicameral mind*, it is only the 'Parent' (P) to 'Child' (C) relationship that exists between the 'Input-provider' and the 'Output-producer' because of the absence of 'consciousness' and 'free will' or 'volition'. The moment 'consciousness' and 'volition' prevail in the post-*bicameral* era, the Ego-states of the parties involved become active and those may be quite different under different circumstances, leading to overt and covert conflicts. That is why, in contemporary world, democracy may be quite a farce. *(Reference 4)*

The Robot Inside You

What all things you do without being 'conscious'? If you try to think of it, you'll be amazed that you'll find too short a list of things that you do consciously. Possibly, the ratio would be 80 (unconscious): 20 (conscious). You are, therefore, 80 percent 'robotic' and only 20 percent 'human', like the 90:10 proportion between the microbial genes and the human genes you have. When you're driving a car, specially on a multi-lane highway, you perform with very little consciousness. In fact, on such occasions, your consciousness would be engaged on something or somewhere else. That is somewhat similar to what happens to a *bicameral* man. He is following something literally which he had not planned or decided himself – which was done at a different place by someone different from him. In case something totally unexpected happens which had not been anticipated, he will wait until he gets instruction from that different place which is the admonitory wisdom of his own life stored inside his own brain. He has to retrieve it 'consciously'.

Hearing Voices

Psychotics, schizophrenics and some epileptics hear voices; they have 'auditory hallucinations' which are much more frequent than the 'visual' ones. Wherefrom such voices come? Do they come from the outside or inside of the patient? It is a mystery to me.

Voices can be heard by many completely normal people to varying degrees. Cases are not rare when a child under 'stress' suddenly hears a parent's comforting voice. In *bicameral* civilisations, voices were often heard by normal people. Such voices were recognized as coming from gods, angels, devils, enemies, or a paternalistic person, an ancestor, or a well-wisher relative.

Auditory or visual hallucinations can take place at times of acute stress or anxiety [like when Sri Sri Ramakrishna used to behave madly to get the vision (*darshan*) of Goddess Kali, or when Chaitanya Mahaprabhu would be desperate to be united with the Dark God Sri Krishna]. However, such anxiety or stress threshold varies from person to person. In the case of persons who have a lower threshold, the build-up in the blood of breakdown products of stress-produced *adrenalin*, the individual would be, for genetic reasons, unable to pass through the kidneys as fast as a normal person.

In the *bicameral mind* era, the stress threshold for hallucinations was much lower than in either normal people or schizophrenics and psychotics today. The only stress necessary was some occasions which could not be managed by the 'robot inside' designed to handle 'routine' situations, when a change in behaviour was necessary because of some novelty in a situation not to be dealt with on the basis of 'habit', any conflict between work and exhaustion, between fight and flight, any choice between whom to obey or what to do, anything that required any decision at all was good enough to cause an auditory hallucination, which was so common.

A Live Case Study: St. Padre Pio

Pio of Pietreicina, widely known as Padre Pio (1887–1968), was an Italian friar, priest and mystic. He used to have apparitions from a very young age. The available records indicate that Padre Pio heard God's voice, particularly as an insistent call "to sacrifice and immolate himself for his brethren". He also experienced other divine communications such as visions and the *stigmata,* and dedicated his life to serving God and guiding others. Padre Pio used these divine communications to grow in his relationship with God and to understand God's will more clearly. The *stigmata*, which appeared in 1918, were another manifestation of his deep spiritual connection with Christ's passion and suffering.

Read Padre Pio's own comments regarding his experience of hearing God's voice:

> "This morning after Mass while I was feeling quite troubled about this matter I was suddenly seized by a violent headache and there and then it seemed to me impossible to continue my thanksgiving.
>
> This condition increased my torment. Moreover, a great aridity invaded my soul and who knows what might not have happened if what I am about to tell you had not taken place.

Our Lord appeared and spoke to me as follows:

> 'My son, do not fail to write down what you hear today from my lips, so that you may not forget it. I am faithful and no creature will be lost unwittingly. Light is very different from darkness. I invariably attract to myself the soul to whom I am accustomed to speak. On the contrary, the wiles of the devil tend to separate it from me. I never inspire in the soul any fears which drive it away from me, the devil never places in the soul any fears which induce it to draw near to me.
>
> If the fears which the soul feels at certain moments of its life on the score of its eternal salvation proceed from me, they can be recognized by the peace and serenity they leave in the soul.'
>
> This vision and locution of Our Lord plunged my soul into such peace and happiness that all the sweetness of the world appears tasteless in comparison to even a single drop of this bliss."

Our soul has two parts – upper and lower. The upper part of our soul is more oriented to our relationship with God, whereas the lower part is orientated to our relationship with this world and to material and temporal circumstances. Any message from the Lord is especially directed towards the upper part of the soul whereas Devil touches more often the lower and more sensual part of the soul.

"I waited patiently to the LORD, and HE inclined to me, and heard my Cry. Waiting patiently in the LORD is key to a VIRTUOUS Life." (PSALM 40.1)

Read the following prayer of Padre Pio addressed to Lord Jesus and see how he invites God to be with him all the time. Is this not the *bicameral mind* approach?

> "Stay with me, Lord....For it's necessary to have you present so that I do not forget you.
>
> You know how easily I abandon you.
>
> Stay with me, Lord because I'm weak and I need your strength, so that I do not fall so often.
> Stay with me, Lord for you are my life and without you I am without fervour.
> Stay with me Lord for you are my light...And without you, I am in darkness
> Stay with me, Lord to show me your will
> Stay with me, Lord so that I hear your voice and follow you
> Stay with me, Lord for I desire to love you very much – and always be in your company.
> Stay with me, Lord if you wish me to be faithful to you
> Stay with me, Lord for us, poor as my soul is – I want to be a place of consolation for you..

A nest of love

Stay with me, Lord for it is getting late.....And the day is coming to a close and life passes.

Death, Judgement, Eternity approaches

It is necessary to renew my strength so that I'll not stop along the way

And for that I need you
It is getting late and death approaches

I fear the darkness, the temptations, the dryness, the cross, the sorrow

Oh, how I need you my Jesus in this night of my exile

Stay with me tonight.

Jesus, in life with all its dangers, I need you.

Let me recognize you as your disciples did at the breaking of the bread so that the

Eucharistic communion may be the light which disperses the darkness—the force with which sustains me, the unique joy of my heart.

Stay with me, Lord because at the hour of my death I want to remain united with you

If not by communion – at least by grace and love.

Stay with me, Jesus I do not ask for divine consolation because I do not merit it

But the gift of your presence, I ask this of you

Stay with me, for it is you alone I look for your love, your grace, your will, your heart, your spirit

Because I love you most and ask for no other reward ....but to love you more and more

With affirm love I will love you with all my heart while on earth and continue to love you perfectly during all eternity!

Amen!!!" *(References 5-8)*

Live Case Study 2: Benoite Rencurel

Author Michael Frez argues that Catholic practices such as 'Eucharistic adoration', 'rosary devotions' (silent devotional chanting) and 'contemplative meditation' with a focus on interior life, facilitate *visions* and *apparitions* as those practices produce an 'Altered State of Consciousness' ('ASC').

Benoite Rencurel (1647–1718) was from the Southern Alps region of France. As she had lost her father at a very early age, she never learnt to read or write although she had a gift of reading hearts. For her livelihood, she took up the job of a shepherdess. She is said to have *stigmata* from birth and have seen apparitions of the Virgin Mary from 1664 to 1718 from the age of 17 till her death. She had also experienced *vision* of Christ bleeding on the village cross. Her apparitions became known as *Our Lady of Laus* and the site receives thousands of pilgrims visiting every year.

The modern message of Benoite is: to live heart to heart with God in prayer, enter deeper into conversation when we are reconciled with ourselves with others and with God, live your life's mission in everyday community and joy. *(References 9-11)*

References

1. 'Eric Berne' – *Wikipedia.*
2. Eric Berne, *Games People Play: The Basic Handbook of Transactional Analysis*, London: Penguin, 2016.
3. Thomas Anthony Harris, *I'm OK, You're OK,* London: Arrow Books, 1995.
4. "Rastafari" – *Wikipedia.*
5. "Padre Pio" – *Wikipedia.*
6. Fray Guillermo Trauba, Capuchin, "Discerning the Voice of the Lord: Insights from Padre Pio's Testimony", *Capuchin Franciscans,* Western America Province, 11th September 2023.
7. Father Ernest Paone, "Padre Pio was in contact with God" *"Padre Pio: Devotions: Post Navigation"*, padrepiodevotions.org
8. "Rare blessing video of Saint Padre Pio and Prayer – audiotape" YouTube Video Presentation, '*Inspiring Prayer*' Channel.
9. "Michael Frez" – *Wikipedia.*
10. "Altered State of Consciousness" – *Wikipedia.*
11. "Benoite Rencurel" – *Wikipedia.*

CHAPTER 8

Hearing Voices

Voice Hearing

The written record of Western history stretches back more than 2,500 years, and from the beginning *voice hearing* was plainly apparent and positively valued. Indeed, the phenomenon is associated with some fundamental texts and figures of Western culture. For example, the ancient Greek epic the *Iliad* – composed around 750 BCE and one of the oldest examples of European literature – is rife with *voices*. Even the great philosopher Socrates heard a *daimonion* – a 'divine thing'. This voice offered the great philosopher simple guidelines with regard to everyday tasks.

In the history of monotheistic religion, *voice-hearing* is even more formative than it was in ancient Greece – literally so. The god of the ancient Hebrews is a god who speaks almost without pause. The book of *Genesis* proclaims: "In the beginning ....God said 'Let there be light', and from that moment forward Yahweh's voice becomes the motive force behind the history of the Jews. It is the divine voice that sets monotheism on its way when it orders Abraham to leave his home and make a 'great nation'. It is the divine voice that orders Abraham to sacrifice his son Isaac and then stays his hand before committing the crime, that respects the blessing of fruitfulness and renown to Isaac and to Jacob, that leads Moses through the desert and delivers to him the laws of Israel. And, it is the divine voice that speaks to all the biblical prophets – from Isaiah to Malachi – and compels them, not without trouble, to carry the divine message to their countrymen.

In Christian theology, Jesus Christ does not hear the word of God – he is the word of God, but all other Saints did. The preacher and author John Benyan and the poets John Milton and William Blake did. But somewhere around the eighteenth century, the culture's way of thinking and talking about unusual experiences altered markedly. What was once revelation and inspiration became symptoms of abnormal behaviour and pathology.

Voice-hearing in the Greek Epic *Iliad*

The most powerful and prideful Agamemnon – the leader of the expedition to Troy, in the tenth year of the Trojan War, announced to the strongest warrior and Greek hero Achilles that he planned to rob him of his bride. This was in retribution for supporting the return of a woman Agamemnon had taken from a local priest. Enraged, Achilles set out to do what he would normally do in such situations: slaughter his challenger and everyone in his path.

Just as Achilles was pulling his sword from his scabbard, the goddess Athena, protector of the Greeks, descended from the heavens to placate his wrath and coax him onto a more prudent path. The goddess stood behind Achilles, appearing to him only and none else could see her. She was invisible to all others. (Does it mean that the goddess Athena had given Achilles the power of the *Third Eye* so that he can see her and hear her voice clearly?)

The goddess now said: "I have come down from the sky to stay your anger. The goddess of the white arms Hera has sent me – who loves both of you equally in her heart and cares for you. Come then, do not take out your sword, keep clear of fighting."

Achilles, uncharacteristically but wisely, took Athena's advice and did not seek his revenge.

In this context, let me introduce to you the reputed Canadian psychiatrist late Dr Eric Berne's 'Transactional Analysis' (TA) concept. Dr Berne had a roaring practice as a psychiatrist and he used to document his patient data meticulously and, whenever he got a little free time, he would analyse them to ascertain if he could find any pattern emerging, and he came up with his theory. He observed that there is a 'Child' (C) ego-state in each individual from the time of his birth. (C) is simple and straightforward. There are two types of (C) – one is most submissive and obedient (OC) who follows without any hassle; follows whom – follows someone who is an 'authority' type – Berne assigned the 'Parent' (P) ego-state to him. There are, once again, two types of (P) ego-states. One is very strict, authoritarian, disciplinarian – whom Berne called 'Critical Parent' (CP) who is without any soft corner. The other one is having a soft corner – benevolent, kind-hearted, permissive, forgiving – the 'Nurturing Parent' (NP). When either a (CP) or an (NP) is interacting with an (OC) there is no problem, the relationship is most smooth and congenial. The situation changes and poses a problem when the (C) is of a different type – argumentative, unreasonable, disobedient – whom Berne described as having a 'Rebellious Child' (RC) ego-state. (OC) is a blind follower, where (RC) is a challenger, a disbeliever.

In the case that I have cited above where goddess Athena is instructing warrior Achilles to put his sword back into its sheath, Athena communicates from her (P) ego-state and Achilles takes her message from his (OC) ego state and follows her instruction without any hassle, although otherwise being a top warrior and a Greek hero, he operated from is (P) ego-state.

In a subsequent chapter where I would be talking about the Jewish prophet Moses and his transactions with the Abrahamic God, when Moses did not have his first son circumcised he behaved like a 'Rebellious Child' (RC) and the God who wanted to take him to task, behaved like a 'Critical Parent' (CP), but fortunately Moses's wife got the circumcision done by operating from her (OC) ego-state and persuaded God to forgive him by behaving like an 'NP'.

God of the Abrahamic Religions: Real or Imaginary

Science does not have the processes to prove or disprove the existence of any God. Science studies and attempts to explain only the natural world while God, in most religions, is supernatural.

In science, explanations are based on evidence drawn from observing the natural world and conducting experiments. Because these explanations are based on evidence, they can be checked independently by others. Religious beliefs do not depend only on empirical evidence. They can also be based on faith and typically involve supernatural forces and entities. Science can't examine or explain the purpose of the universe. That's a question that falls under theology or philosophy.

Now, God of the Abrahamic religions: real or imaginary?

This is a philosophical question with no single, universally accepted answer. The determination of whether the God of the Abrahamic religion is 'real or imaginary' depends on one's perspective, belief system and methodology of determining truth.

For believers in Abrahamic religions, God is a real, eternal, omnipotent, and omniscient entity who created the universe. For them, belief is a matter of faith, not empirical evidence. Their conviction is based on spiritual experiences, revelation through scriptures (such as the Torah, Bible, and Quran) and personal convictions.

In Judaism and Islam, God is seen as a singular indivisible being. In mainstream Christianity, God is understood as a Holy Trinity of three divine powers: the Father, the Son, and the Holy Spirit.

Religious texts like the Quran state that no vision can grasp God, but that God's grasp is over all visions. Abrahamic faiths believe God revealed himself to prophets like Abraham, Moses, and Muhammad. Miracles and personal spiritual experiences are considered proof of God's existence and involvement in the world. God is believed to exist outside of space and time but is also personal and involved in the world, listening to prayers and reacting to the actions of humanity. *(References 1-5)*

References

1. "Does Science Disprove the Existence of God?" *The Science Behind the Culture of Science*, National Academy of Sciences.
2. Daniel Smith, *Muses, Madmen and Prophets: Rethinking the History, Science and Meaning of Auditory Hallucination*, New York: The Penguin Press, 2007.

3. "Eric Berne" – *Wikipedia.*
4. Eric Berne, *Games People Play: The Psychology of Human Relationships*, London: Penguin Books, 1964.
5. Eric Berne, *What Do You Say After You Say Hello? The Psychology of Human Destiny,* London: Corgi Ed. Andre Deutsch Ltd., 1975.

CHAPTER 9

Hallucinations & Dopamine

"......the hallucination provided a peculiarly human model. Hallucinations in other animals, if they occur, are very difficult to ascertain and evaluate. But many important human experiences (such as the dreams and visions of biblical prophets and the creative imagery of great artists) are not only related to hallucinations, but also deeply bound into the history and cultural experience of mankind."

—**L. J. West MD**

In: *Hallucinations: Behaviour, Experiences and Theory* (Preface)

Ed. R. K. Siegel and L. J. West
New York: John Wiley and Sons, 1975

Hallucinations

Hallucinations are sensory experiences (seeing, hearing, tasting, smelling, or feeling things that are not there); while 'delusions' are fixed, false, unshakable beliefs that persist despite evidence to the contrary. The easily available 'feel good' brain chemical *Dopamine* (D) is strongly linked to 'hallucinations' (both 'visual' and 'auditory') and 'delusions'.

The brain's mesolimbic pathway is a crucial neural circuit that transmits 'D' from the midbrain's 'Ventral Tegmental Area' ('VTA') to the limbic system, particularly the 'Nucleus Accumbens', playing a central role in reward motivation. When a rewarding stimulus is encountered, this pathway is activated, leading to the release of 'D'. Excessive 'D' activity in the brain's mesolimbic pathway is thought to cause 'object-seeing' (visual hallucination) and 'voice-hearing' (auditory hallucination).

An excess of 'D' in certain brain areas can lead to hallucinations; while a lack of 'D' in other areas can contribute to negative symptoms like lack of motivation and drive. 'D' dysregulation can also cause a perceptual bias towards internal expectations over external sensory evidence, a mechanism believed to underpin hallucinations in conditions like schizophrenia. Hallucinations are the outcome of self (or, internally)-created satisfaction of 'D' hunger. Routine activities do not lead to the release of 'D'. So, the brain hallucinates to earn 'D'.

Excessive 'D' release may lead to 'aberrant salience', where the brain incorrectly attaches high importance to random stimuli, potentially leading to false beliefs (delusions) and misperception (hallucination).

Expectation of 'Hallucination'

In normal perception, predictive interpretations of forthcoming sensory input are formed in the pre-frontal areas of the brain's cerebral cortex and communicated to the sensory cortex. In auditory hallucination, the predictions of predictive input are relatively unconstrained by predictive error and erroneously identified as representation of actual auditory signal evoked by external stimulation. This is the 'key' process leading to the experience of hallucination.

'Expectation' of hallucination refers to the role of strong prior beliefs and internal 'expectations' in creating these sensory experiences, as described by the predictive processing framework of the brain.

The brain constantly forms predictive models of the world based on past experiences and prior beliefs. When incoming sensory data does not match the internal predictions, a 'prediction error' is identified. Hallucinations can occur when these 'prediction errors' are misinterpreted, leading the brain to process an internal, unconstrained prediction as a real sensory experience. In hallucinations, there is an imbalance where 'expectations' driven by strong prior beliefs can become stronger than the reliability of external sensory information. Dysfunction in brain regions like the 'Pre-Frontal Cortex' and 'Auditory Cortex', along with issues with the neurotransmitter system, can contribute to this imbalance and the generation of hallucination.

The brain constantly makes 'predictions' (which form the bases of 'expectations'), and the ability to accurately distinguish between such predictions by the brain and the external reality is crucial for normal perception. The 'expectation'-based approach emphasizes how learning and inference play active role in the genesis of 'hallucination'.

Both healthy individuals and psychotic patients who experience daily hallucinations have been found to over-rely on prior perceptions and expectations of sensory information. *(References 1-5)*

References

1. Christoph Teufel, "Sensory Neuroscience: Linking, Dopamine, Expectation, and Hallucination", *Current Biology*, Vol. 28, Issue 4, 19th February 2018, pp. R158–R160.
2. Franciska de Beer, "Hallucinations & Expectations: The influence of expectations on perception in relation to hallucination-proneness" Master's Thesis in Behavioural and Cognitive Neurosciences, Faculty of Science and Engineering, University of Groningen, 12th July 2020.
3. Clifford M. Cassidy *et al.*, "A perceptual inference mechanism for hallucination linked to striatal dopamine", *Current Biology*, February 2018, Vol. 28, No. 4, pp. 503–514.
4. J. M. Nazimek, M.D. Hunter, P.W.R. Woodruff, "Auditory Hallucination: Expectation-perception model", *Medical Hypotheses*, Vol. 78, Issue 6, June 2012, pp. 802–810.
5. "Hallucinations" – *Cleveland Clinic.*

CHAPTER 10

The Bicameral Mind

(Gods as Aids for Living & Working)

Mind

> "They searched and searched, searched some more - it just kept disappearing.
>
> After all that search, when they couldn't find it they gave up and said: 'Beyond'."

This poem is by Sant Kabir (1398–1518), the Indian devotional mystical poet. Pre-historic men and many mystics, spiritual masters, prophets, and avatars have been **hearing voices** (having auditory hallucinations) as they were having *bicameral minds* – their brain's left side (output-producer) being used for day-to-day survival-oriented routine living and working and the right side (input-provider) getting involved in non-routine, challenging situations, like a complex problem-solving, conflict management or making choices from available alternatives. I surmise that those voice-hearers would go on searching for the sources of such voices and finally would give up, not knowing that the voices were coming from within their own minds – their brains' right hemispheres. This is my interpretation of this charming couplet (*doha*), translated by Linda Hess and Shukdev Singh.

'Passengers': People without Any Ambitions, Aspirations & Drive

It is not rare to find many of our contemporaries even today in whom ambitions, aspirations and drives do not stem out from their own minds unless they are provoked by someone from outside. They are just passing their time as 'passengers' on this planet, called earth. This is the propensity inherited from our very remote ancestors like the ancient Greeks (3,000 to 4,000 years ago) whose emotions and desires originated as consequences of actions of gods external to themselves, as had been proposed by the American psychologist Julian Jaynes (1920–1997).

According to Jaynes's theory, such 'passengers' (as I call them) have no *'consciousness'* as such – as they have no 'free will' or 'volition'. For such people, lacking in 'free will', the human mind's functions are divided into two halves of the brain – one part is the 'speaking' part and the other part is the 'listening' part. The former issues instructions, commands, guidance and directions whereas the latter follows, obeys, implements, and acts. Jaynes described such minds as *Bicameral Minds* – minds having two chambers or rooms. In such minds, *consciousness* does not develop if *Bicameralism* did not break down. To quote James: "........at one time, human nature was split into two: an 'executive' part called a *god*, and a 'follower' part, called a *man"*.

Jaynes had proposed that the experiences and memories of the right hemisphere of the brain were transmitted to the left hemisphere via auditory hallucinations. The metaphor is not meant to imply that the two halves of the brain were cut off from each other but in the case of bicameral functioning, any novel, non-routine stimuli would be mediated through a linguistic control mechanism and expressed as auditory hallucination.

Dependence on Gods

The ancient gods were not fictitious characters. They had origins in the nervous systems of early humans. In ancient civilisations like Mesopotamia, Egypt and Indus Valley, gods and goddesses existed in different forms as deities in god-houses. However, personal gods also existed as hallucinatory voices originating from the right hemisphere of the brain. These voices used a language to condense some important information into a message which can change the passive behaviour in response to a novel stimulus eventually. To my mind, ancient people who used to feel insecure, helpless and incapable to cope with non-routine situations, used to depend on gods and goddesses in prayer-houses as well as imaginary personal gods inside their brains, as aids for living and working.

Such dependence on gods was gradually replaced by 'self-confidence' when ancient men were compelled to use their free will to decide on courses of actions for handling unprecedented situations as auditory hallucinations were not readily available to common men. The gods preferred messengers like Abraham, Moses, Muhammad and such other spiritually developed persons through whom the sacred texts were transmitted. This 'self-confidence' I would describe as 'Ego' with a positive tone ('I Can' and 'I Will'). This state of mind is what, I suppose, Jaynes describes as *consciousness*.

Bicameral mind cannot reason. It lacks meta-consciousness, autobiographical memory, and capacity for executive *ego-functions* such as brainstorming, deliberate mind wandering and conscious introspection of mental content. *Bicameral mentality* was a method of *social control* in simple social groups having up to 100 members, and when it did not work in complex civilisations, the mental model was replaced by the *conscious* mode of thought, which is grounded in the acquisition of *metaphorical language*, which came into use for inter-personal and social communication.

Similar to Schizophrenic Mind

Bicameral people experienced the world in a manner that has some similarity to a person with schizophrenia. Rather than making *conscious* evaluation in novel or totally unexpected, unprecedented situations, the person hallucinated a voice or *god* giving admonitory advice or commands and obeyed without questions. One was not at all conscious of one's own thought-processes *per se*.

Ancient Greek Psychology

Ancient Greeks may have known that an individual did things, but the reason – why they did things was attributed to divine externalities, such as *gods* or *demons*. There was no sense of 'self' in the modern sense. Greek civilisation developed ego-centred psychology as an adaptation to living in city-states.

Split Brain Research

Jaynes's model has found support from neuroscientists Roger Sperry and Michael Gazzanigga's split-brain experiments. Based on such split-brain research data, Jaynes inferred that the 'voices' came from the right brain counterparts of the left brain language centres, specifically the counterparts to Wernicke's area in the 'temporal lobe' and Broca's area in the 'frontal lobe'. These areas are somewhat dormant in the right brains of most modern humans but some studies show that auditory hallucination correspond to increased activity in these areas of the brain. The right brain's corresponding regions contribute to language processing by interpreting the emotional context, understanding spatial relationship in language, and processing broader aspects of language rather than its literal meaning and production. The right hemisphere also plays a crucial role in understanding commands involving the entire body and maintaining a comprehensive view of spoken communication. Jaynes argues that people with schizophrenia feel a loss of identity due to hallucinated voices taking the place of their internal monologue.

Hearing Voices: Hallucinations

Elizabeth Donaldson's Experience

"Get away from there! Leave! Leave immediately!" It was 3 am and Elizabeth Donaldson woke to the sound of her mother screaming at her apartment door. The old lady had heard voices of people – taunts, threats from her neighbours in the adjoining apartments and their friends. Elizabeth asked her if she could open the door to show her that nobody was there. But to her those were not just voices, they were real. One of the most frustrating and disempowering aspects of her auditory hallucination is that she does not recognise them as hallucinations (in psychiatry, this is called a lack of 'insight'). Opening the door and finding the entrance lobby empty would not have brought her peace as she would have believed that because the bad people heard Elizabeth and her mother walking toward the door, they would have run back into their respective apartments. After all, she could still hear the murmuring behind the closed doors of their apartments. For Elizabeth's mother, this paranoid schizophrenia was most disturbing and needed medical intervention.

Daniel Smith's Experience

Daniel B. Smith is also a child of a person who heard voices, and his book *Muses, Madmen and Prophets: Rethinking the History, Science and Meaning of Auditory Hallucination*, is in part an effort to understand, his family's experience with voice hearing. Smith first became aware of his father's voices when he and his brother were helping their grandfather put together a self-published memoir. In a short piece called "Voices", his grandfather described hearing voices that helped him make decisions, take exams, and even play cards. For Smith's grandfather, the voices he heard were helpful and non-threatening, required attention and patience to hear and were seemingly never a cause of anxiety or shame. For Smith's father, however, the voices he heard, although similarly non-threatening, were commanding and intrusive, difficult to ignore, and a source of deep shame and concern. Smith's father felt betrayed by his own father's silence regarding these voices, he 'felt that he had been denied his salvation'. Had Smith's father known earlier that it was possible to live comfortably with voices, perhaps his life would have been easier.

Surya's Experience (from the 2024-25 Bengali Movie Dabadu*)*

Young Surya grows up in the slums of North Kolkata, India. He discovers chess through his supportive grandfather, Nabin Sarkar, despite facing poverty and opposition from his alcoholic father. Surya's mother, Karuna Devi becomes his main supporter as he pursues his passion for chess. As Surya navigates the competitive chess scene, he trains under two contrasting coaches: the encouraging Rathindra and later the abusive Samiran. His journey is filled with challenges but he reaches the pinnacle of success because of two main reasons:

first, his zeal and determination; and, last but not the least, the most supporting *audio-visual hallucinations* from his deceased grandfather Nabin Sarkar. Nabin used to appear before and guide him at times of acute crises. Surya became victorious in the 1998 Commonwealth Games Championship at young age of 19 years, making him India's youngest Grandmaster.

How Do We Look at Bicameral Mentality Today

Bicameral mentality was common in ancient times, when groups were small, fixed at one location for years. A shift from *bicameral mentality* marked the beginning of introspection and consciousness. Up to my college and university days in India, I was living with my parents and my grandmother and all my uncles and aunts were living close by and would meet frequently, with some almost every day and my *consciousness* did not develop as it was not allowed to develop. My *consciousness* developed when I went abroad alone for my higher studies at the age of 22. I was in a totally *alien* culture.

Likewise, a shift from *bicameral mentality* took place in the 2nd millennium BCE when mass migrations started – which created a rash of unexpected situations and stresses that required ancient minds to be more flexible, environment-alert and creative. Self-awareness, or *consciousness* was the culturally evolved solution to this problem – as there was no common language for people to discuss, share problems and solutions, or common social upbringing. Thus, *consciousness*, like *bicameral mentality*, emerged as a neurological adaptation to social complexity in a changing world.

As god's voices could not be heard regularly any longer, divination, prayer and oracles arose as new strategies for getting his blessings and directions. The consultation of people having active and operative *bicameral minds* became a common practice.

Leftovers of the *bicameral mind* today, according to Jaynes, are what are regarded as mental illnesses, such as schizophrenia. There is no evidence of insanity existing prior to the breakdown of the *bicameral.* This is an indirect evidence of Jaynes's theory. *(References 1-9)*

References

1. Ed. Arundhathi Subramaniam, *A Book of Bhakti Poetry: Eating God*, Gurugram, UP, India, Penguin Random House India, 2014.
2. Julian Jaynes, *The Origin of Consciousness in the Breakdown of the Bicameral Mind*, Boston: Mariner Books, Houghton & Mifflin, 2000.
3. Peter Sellick, "A Resurgence of Julian Jaynes's Theory of Consciousness", produced by Marcel Kuijsten for the Julian Jaynes Society Podcast, December 2024.
4. "Quantum Consciousness and the Origin of Life" Video Interview with Stuart Hammeroff, *AZPM Channel*, May 2025.
5. "Roger Wolcott Sperry" – *Britannica*, Updated till 16th August 2025.
6. "Michael Gazzanigga" – *Wikipedia.*
7. Daniel B. Smith, *Muses, Madmen and Prophets*, New York: Penguin, 2008.
8. Elizabeth Donaldson, Ph.D., "Review of Daniel B. Smith's *Muses, Madmen and Prophets*, *Metapsychology*, Vol. 11, No. 49.
9. 'Dabadu' – *Wikipedia.*

CHAPTER 11

The Bicameral Brain

The Human Brain: Bicameral

The human brain has two hemispheres. While both hemispheres understand language, in Right-Handed Persons (RHP), it is only the left hemisphere that can speak. There is some 'vestigial' functioning of the right hemisphere' "Wernicke's area" in a way similar to the voice of gods.

['Vestigial Structures' in the human brain are often described as structures or cavities that may have had functions in earlier embryonic or foetal life and are reduced or functionally insignificant in the adult brain. The Right Brain's "Wernicke's area' is responsible for the 'intonation', the 'emphasis' and the 'emotional tone' of speech – the 'musical' part of language.]

The two hemispheres are able to act almost as two independent persons. The right as the 'Input-provider' or 'Instructor' and the left as the 'Output-producer' or 'Follower/Implementor/Executor'. The right is the 'God' and the left is the 'man'.

The Language Areas

For a RHP, the left hemisphere has language areas in the: (i) Broca's area (of medium size) in the frontal lobe; (ii) Supplementary Motor area in the frontal lobe (relatively small); and (iii) Wernicke's area (relatively large in size) in the temporal lobe. It is the last one – the Wernicke's area that is the most indispensable to normal speech. There is no disagreement about its importance to meaningful communication. Most other functions are bilaterally represented. Why the language function be represented in only one hemisphere? Is it because the right hand being the 'working hand', language must be used to represent its various functions essential for daily living and working – like pushing, pulling, cutting, chopping, tearing, shearing, throwing, lifting, keeping, holding, shifting, mixing, screwing, squeezing, kneading, and so on – for all of which hand tools and artifacts evolved over times. Only in exceptional cases, such as in the growing brain of a child or in ambidextrous people, the usually speechless right hemisphere can, under certain conditions, become a language hemisphere just like the left.

What are the functions of the areas of the right hemisphere corresponding to the speech areas of the left? Detailed probing has shown nothing. In fact, large portions of the right hemisphere are simply unnecessary. In fact, large amount of right hemisphere tissue, including what corresponds to Wernicke's area, and even in some cases, the entire hemisphere has been cut out in human patients because of illness or injury with surprisingly little deficit in mental function. Could it be that these silent 'speech' areas on the right hemisphere had some function at an earlier stage in man's history that now they do not have?

The 'God' Concept

The 'God' concept is abstract. Jehovah of the Jews and Allah of the Muslims cannot be seen. Christians are practical in the sense that although their God and Holy Spirit cannot be seen, God's son Lord Jesus has a human form. The Hindu gods and goddesses are entirely imaginary. In fact, one Goddess Kali can have different forms. Imagination and visualisation being faculties of the Right Brain in RHPs, they also have existence in the Right Brain like the abstract Gods Jehovah and Allah. Hindu gods and goddesses and abstract Gods like Jehovah and Allah are worshipped according to their 'qualities' (*gunas*). Lord Jesus, I presume, is in the Left Brain. Although photography had not been invented in Jesus's time, paintings of the Lord are available in hundreds and thousands – many of which were painted in his time.

There has not been any change in modern times from the ancient times. In modern times, the Right Brain is where the Hindu gods and goddesses as well as the abstract Jehovah and Allah live. So it was in ancient times, before the dawn of the language-based civilisation. The Right Brain is thus more important for a theist although the Left Brain is the working brain. Therefore, there is a possibility that theists live their daily life on inaudible commands from gods/goddesses and audible commands and advices by their seniors whom they respect, like parents, grandparents, other family elders, teachers, tutors, professors, gurus. The mantras, chants, hymns, psalms, eulogies (of seniors) all are received in the Right Brain.

Inter-hemispheric Transmission

Obviously, there have to be certain tracts by which inter-hemispheric transmission would be possible. The main connecting bridge tissue *corpus callosum* is too large made of two million fibres, so the private callosum between the two temporal lobes – the much smaller *anterior commissures* are involved in this crucial task.

In ancient times, what corresponds to Wernicke's area on the right hemisphere might have had organised admonitory experience and coded with 'voices' which were then 'heard' over the anterior commissure by the left, or dominant hemisphere.

Obedience to the Voice Heard

Imagine someone speaking to you with a commanding voice, in an authoritarian style. It rings a bell in your memory. You had been an 'Obedient Child' (OC) to your 'Parents' ('Critical' and 'Nurturing'). That childhood experience (when your 'consciousness' had not awakened and you had no 'free will' or 'volition' – you could be easily 'controlled') prompts you to listen to the voice most attentively with your ears totally focused, and follow the command underlying the voice obediently. If you do not obey it in the first instance, the owner of the voice feels that you've not heard him, so he repeats what he had said, and he goes on repeating like a most committed parent until you show signs of obeying it.

Because of man's total reliance and dependence on God in the early periods of human history, the linguistic faculty of men was involved with only one hemisphere in order to leave the other hemisphere free for the voice of gods and god-like figures.

Let us recall what the famous neurosurgeon Wilder Penfield of McGill University, Montreal, Canada experienced in his famous series of 'Awake Brain Surgery' cases.

A twenty-year-old college student, when the Wernicke's area of his right hemisphere was stimulated with very mild electricity, cried out: "Again I hear voices and, when it happens, I sort of lose touch with reality. I get a humming in my ears and a feeling like a warning". Every time, his same brain area was touched, he had the same response.

A twenty-six-year-old housewife, who got stimulated in approximately the same area, had a similar 'voice-hearing' experience. There were quite a few similar experiences of voice-hearing in Penfield's massive study. *(References 1&2)*

Bicameral Hemispheric Difference

The right hemisphere, like the gods, sees parts as having a meaning only within a context; it looks at wholes. While the left or dominant hemisphere, like the man side of the bicameral mind, looks at the parts themselves.

In the bicameral era, what corresponds to Wernicke's area on the right non-dominant hemisphere, had its strict bicameral function, whereas after a couple of thousand years of psychological reorganisation in which such bicameralism was discouraged when it appeared in early development that, such areas functioned in a different way. And, similarly, it would be wrong to think that whatever the neurology of 'consciousness' now may be, is set for all times to come. The function of brain tissue is not fixed or inevitable and perhaps different organisations, given different development programmes, may be possible.

References

1. "Wilder Penfield" – *Wikipedia.*
2. Julian Jaynes, *The Origin of Consciousness in the Breakdown of the Bicameral Mind*, Boston, New York: A Mariner Book, Houghton Mifflin Company, 2000.

CHAPTER 12

Organised Groups

The Leadership Role

Prehistoric men were wild, nomadic – not civilised. By 'civilised', I mean in 'well-organised' groups.

They were living the life of hunter-gatherers – without any agriculture, fisheries, poultry or cattle farming. Their intelligence was limited to the 'present' only – 'catch, kill, eat, and live'. They looked for daily provisions only. They could never think and plan for tomorrow and the day after. They never thought their daily hunting and fruit-gathering could be solved if they could plan how to stock them and how to keep them fresh from rotting. They lacked in planning and organising intelligence. That was even prior to the era of *bicameral minds* with its controlling gods which evolved at the initial stage of the evolution of language. Pre-historic people's language was non-verbal like those of the primates and apes – visual and auditory signals. Visual signals could not be seen in dense forests and in darkness. Such environmental circumstances called for auditory signals. Different types of signals were used for different circumstances. The most common were 'danger calls' and the nature of these calls varied as to whether the danger was imminent and proximal or it was not imminent and distant. Such audio-visual signals are still used by kids when they play hide-and-seek and other games. The pre-language era human brain had the capacity to receive such audio-visual signals in the right hemisphere of the brain. And, there is no wonder that such signals (in the form of visual or auditory hallucinations) are received by many people even today, who are not psychotic, schizophrenic or epileptic.

A human society will be called 'civilised' when a group of people is organised under an effective leadership, where the 'leader' replaces

'God' in the right hemisphere of those who are led by the leader. On many critical, non-routine situations, the leader becomes the 'Input-provider' and the led become the 'output-producers'.

Ezekiel's Vision

The Abrahamic religions acknowledge Ezekiel as a prophet. An Israelite priest, he had prophesized the destruction of Judah's the capital city of Jerusalem. In 587 BC, the Neo-Babylonian Empire conquered Jerusalem, destroyed the Solomon's temple, and sent the Judahite upper classes into the Babylonian captivity. He had also prophesized the eventual restoration of the Jewish people to the Land of Israel.

Ezekiel saw a vision of a throne chariot, a symbol of God's majestic presence and power. The chariot that he saw was supported by four-winged, fair-faced living creatures (identified as *cherubim*) and accompanied by complex eye-covered wheels. The cherubim's four faces were those of a man, a lion, an ox, and an eagle – representing different aspects of creation. They also had four wings that allowed them to move swiftly in any direction.

Above the cherubim, on a brilliant sapphire throne sat a radiant figure described as the appearance of the likeness of the glory of the Lord, surrounded by light like that of a rainbow. The *Book of Ezekiel* relating to Ezekiel's vision and acts is named after him. *(Reference 1)*

Moses and God's Law

In Abrahamic religions, Moses was the Hebrew prophet who led the Israelites out of slavery in the Exodus from Egypt. He is considered the most important prophet in Judaism and in Samaritanism and one of the most important prophets in Christianity, Islam, the Bahai Faith, and other Abrahamic religions. According to both the Bible and the Quran, God dictated the Mosaic Law ti Moses, which he wrote down in the five books of the Torah.

Born of Hebrew parents, Moses was brought by the Egyptian Pharaoh's daughter in the royal family. After killing an Egyptian slave-master who was beating a Hebrew, Moses fled across the Red Sea to a place where he encountered the Angel of the Lord, speaking to him from within a burning bush on Mount Hareb. God sent him back to Egypt to demand the release of the Israelites from slavery. He led the Exodus of the Israelites out of Egypt and across the Red Sea, after which they based themselves at Mount Sinai when he received the Ten Commandments. After 40 years of wandering in the desert, Moses died on Mount Nebo at the age of 120, within sight of the Promised Land.

God had threatened to disturb Moses's family peace by making his son Gershom suddenly ill because Moses had not circumcised his son, which was a breach of covenant with Abraham and a failure to keep his own household in order, making him unfit to be a spiritual leader for Israel. Moses's wife Zipporah, intervened by performing the circumcision and the threat subsided allowing Moses to continue his mission to lead the Israelites out of Egypt.

God calls for total obedience and righteousness, even in the small details of daily life. *(References 2&3)*

The Case Study of Joan of Arc

Joan (1412–1431) was born to a propertied peasant family in north-east France. At the age of 16, she requested to be taken to the Charles VII, testifying that she was guided by *visions* from the archangel Michael, Saint Margaret and Saint Catherine to help him save France from English domination. Convinced of her purity, devotion, and patriotism, Charles sent Joan to Orleans as part of a relief army. She arrived at the city in April 1429, displaying her *leadership*, and brought hope to the demoralised French army. Nine days after her arrival, the English abandoned the siege. Joan exercised her leadership quality and encouraged the French to fight against the English which resulted in another victory and Charles was crowned as the King of France with Joan by his side. These victories boosted French morale, paving the way for their final triumph on the Hundred Years' War several decades later.

After Charles's coronation, Joan participated in the unsuccessful siege of Paris and the failed siege of La Charite. Thereafter, she failed in her attempt to relieve Compiegne from the Burgundians but she was captured and ultimately handed over to the English. She was put on trial, declared guilty of blasphemy and demonic visions and burned to death at the stake in 1431, aged about nineteen. In 1456, a reinvestigation overturned the verdict, declaring that it was tainted by deceit and procedural errors. She was described as an obedient member of the Catholic Church, an early feminist, and a symbol of freedom and independence. She is popularly revered as a martyr. In 1922, she was declared one of the patron saints of France.

Modern scholars have discussed possible neurological and psychiatric causes for her *visions*. Her *visions* have been described as hallucinations arising from *epilepsy* or a *temporal lobe tuberculoma*.

Others have implicated *ergot poisoning*, *schizophrenia,* or *delusional disorder* or *creative psychopathy,* induced by her early childhood rearing. However, Joan's firm belief in the divinity of her visions strengthened her confidence, enabled her to trust herself and gave her hope during her capture and trial. *(References 4&5)*

The Mesolithic Era

Travel back to 10,000 to 8,000 BC. During this period, the environment was post-glacial. Man takes to hunting on plain grasslands and forests, to the collection of shellfish and other marine resources. The human brain's 'Seeking Circuit' ('EEL': Explore-Experiment-Learn) became most active. After a few decades of trial, it got permanently fixed in the human brain.

Populations also got stabilised and lifespan of members started becoming longer. With all such developments, there was an imminent need for specific *identity* of the members of any social group. Even today, for how long can a little kid be referred to as 'baby' or 'kiddie' or 'munna' or 'munni'? Those are too general. Use of a 'noun-based name' makes the relationship much more intense.

Even, in the case of auditory hallucinations, if the 'speaker' discloses his identity by mentioning his name (as it had happened in the case of Moses and Muhammad hearing voices), such interactions assume a greater importance for the 'follower's behaviour. The Mesolithic Age (around 8,000 BC in Europe) witnessed the beginnings of animal domestication and, later, agriculture. However, it was still pre-historic times, leading from the 'Paleolithic' age of pure hunting and gathering, characterized by the use of rudimentary chipped stone tools. The change from a hunting-gathering economy to a food-producing economy was the gigantic step leading to the dawn of civilisation. A site has been excavated in Israel, where the hunter Natufians lived initially in the mouths of caves. They used to practice cave art and wore perforated shells or animal teeth as ornaments. In course of time, their future generations left leaving in caves and started living in permanent townships each having at least 200 persons. Three successive permanent towns have been excavated, dating from about 9,000 BC. The inhabitants used most primitive forms of agriculture and a variety of animal fauna was the significant part of their diet.

The Natufians were not 'conscious' people. They were guided entirely by the most elementary *'Stimulus-Response (S-R)'* principle which involved responding to stimuli minute-to-minute. It is also not unlikely that they did not have effective leaders who could interact with 200 people regularly, keep them motivated and help them taking decisions and solving their difficult problems. Even for the most effective leader, it is impossible to be in regular touch with more than six to seven people – 200 is too large a number which requires a hierarchical organisation like in the primate and ape societies.

Under such circumstances, the *hallucinated voice* would have been a very effective 'cohesive' factor for the entire group of 200 people. The voice would have been heard by each of them separately. And, in an ancient civilisation which was a kingdom having a king, the voice was that of the king and it said something which the king had never said or used to say. The voice-receiver's or voice-listener's brain created the input as he knew what the input-producer would have said. Thus, each worker in the field, busy collecting his day's consumables by gathering shellfish or catching small games or planting seed or engaged in a quarrel with a co-worker had within him a 'voice' of his King to **lead** the group in absentia. In the case of a spiritually inclined person, it was the voice of an Angel or God.

Voices of such 'authority' represented human volition as the *bicameral men* did not have their own volitions. Brain's right hemisphere was the 'speaker' and the working left hemisphere was the 'follower'. The 'speaker' gave orders, instructions, warnings, and made prophecies. The medium of transmission of the messages became the 'language' of that culture.

The hypothesis as above may be brought together as five observations: (1) that both hemispheres of the brain are able to understand language, while normally only the left can speak; (2) that there is some vestigial functioning of the right hemisphere's Wernicke's area in a way similar to the voice of some 'authority figure' like God; (3) that the two hemispheres, under certain conditions are able to act almost as independent persons, their relationship corresponding to that of the man-God relationship of *bicameral* times; (4) that contemporary differences between the two hemispheres in cognitive functions at least echo such differences of function between man and God as seen in the literature of *bicameral men;* and, (5) that the brain is more capable of being organised by the environment than we have hitherto supposed, and therefore, would have undergone such a change as from *bicameral* to *conscious* man mostly on the basis of learning and culture.

Mortification: Teresa of Avila

In the Catholic context, mortification is a spiritual practice of *self-denial* and discipline to 'put to death' sinful desires and tendencies, with the goal of growing closer to God. Jesus Christ had called for his followers to 'deny themselves' and 'take up their cross'.

Teresa Sanchez de Cepeda Davila y Ahumada was born in a place called Avila in Spain in 1515. In 1534, she decided to enter the local easy-going Carmelite Convent of the Incarnation. Reading of mystical literature, she became zealous for 'mortification' which caused her to become ill and she spent almost a year in bed. She nearly died but she recovered, attributing her recovery to the miraculous intercession of Saint Joseph. She began to experience bouts of religious *ecstasy,* during which she had perceived 'perfect union with God'. In 1559, she became firmly convinced that Jesus Christ had presented himself to her in bodily form, though invisible. In one *vision*, she says (to quote her own words):

"I saw in his hand a long spear of gold, and at the point there seemed to be a little fire. He appeared to me to be thrusting it at times into my heart, and to pierce my very entrails; when he drew them out also, and to leave me all on fire with a great love of God. The pain was so great, that it made me moan; and yet so surpassing was the sweetness of this excessive pain, that I could not wish to be rid of it..."

The memory of this episode served as an inspiration throughout the rest of her life. The following adage is often associated with her: "Lord, either let me suffer or let me die".

Subsequently, neurologists and psychiatrists have speculated that she might had suffered from *temporal lobe epilepsy.*

Teresa was bombarded with supernatural experiences and visions. Jesus once said to her in a vision:

> "I would create the universe again just to hear you say that you love me".

An episode famous in Teresa's life is worth a mention. Her little nephew was crushed by the wall of a new structure which fell on him as he was playing, and he was carried, apparently lifeless, to Teresa. She held the child in her arms and prayed. After some minutes, she restored him alive and transferred him to his most anxious grief-stricken mother. *(References 6&7)*

Note for the Reader

Do not go for a god or a goddess which has a form and is all dressed and decked up. Go for a formless God, which represents 'mortification'. By practising 'mortification', you will automatically be moving closer to

God. If you are 'mortified' with absolutely plain, simple and frugal living, you need not attach importance to the god-corner or the god-room in your house although you may have one – as you have already developed some godliness in yourself.

Hallucination: Why

The occasion of an hallucination was 'stress' – the 'stress' caused by a person's death; more so, if the person was the binding and cohesive force for the whole group. Even today, the 'stress' may make a schizophrenic hear the voice of someone very high up in the hierarchy – like the Head of the State or the Head of the nation.

As civilisations flourished and cities were formed, the God who was housed in the right hemisphere of the brain of the 'output-producer' was taken out and, in its specific form, was put inside a special holy building – a synagogue, a church, a mosque or a temple. There was such a special building in every locality for every small social groups. Where the God had no special form, its prophets or sacred texts which recorded God's commandments were worshipped. Villages, towns, cities and metros today are God-houses surrounded by man-houses. In many dwelling houses also, like in Hindu houses, there is a god-room, surrounded by man-rooms.

Eyes Speak

Eyes are the index of the mind. Eye-to-eye contact in primates is extremely important. Below humans, it is indicative of the hierarchical position of the animal, the submissive animal turning away grinning in many primate species. But, in humans, perhaps because of the much longer juvenile period, eye-to-eye contact has evolved into a social interaction of great importance. An infant child, when its mother speaks to it, looks at the mother's eyes, not her lips. The response is automatic and universal. The development of such eye-to-eye contact into authority relationships and love relationships is an exceedingly important trajectory that has yet to be traced. It is sufficient here merely to suggest that you are most likely to feel a superior's authority when you and he are staring straight into each other's eyes. There is a kind of *stress*, an unresolvedness about the experience; and without something of a diminution of 'consciousness', so that were such a relationship mimicked in a statue, it would enhance the hallucination of divine speech.

The eyes thus become a prominent feature of most temple statuary throughout the *bicameral* period. The diameter of the human eye is about 10 percent of the height of the head, this proportion being what I shall call the 'eye index' of an idol. In some cases, the idol has huge eyes – eye indices as high as 18 to 20 percent, as in the case of the Hindu God Lord Jagannath.

References

1. 'Ezekiel' – *Wikipedia.*
2. "Moses" – *Wikipedia.*
3. Clement Harrold, "Why does God try to kill Moses in Exodus 4?" *St. Pauls Center*, 3rd May 2024.
4. "Joan of Arc" – *Wikipedia.*
5. "St. Joan of Arc" – *Britannica.*
6. "Teresa of Avila" – *Wikipedia.*
7. "St. Teresa of Avila" – ewtn.com/Catholicism.

CHAPTER 13

End of The Bicameral Era

Breakdown of the Bicameral Mind

The civilisation of Ancient Mesopotamia (modern-day Iraq and Syria) grew up along the banks of two great rivers, the Euphrates and the Tigris. In the midst of a vast desert, the people of Mesopotamia relied upon these rivers to provide drinking water, agricultural irrigation, and major transportation routes. For 3,000 years, the people of Mesopotamia maintained a significant degree of cultural unity, even though politically they were much more fragmented. That was possibly due to the prevalence of the *Bicameral Mind*, which broke down eventually.

Mesopotamia of 1,243 BC! Visualise the imposing walls of ancient Ashur. Thousands of victorious soldiers are marching home. At the head of the Army rides Tukulti-Ninurta I, a king whose towering ambition would reshape the ancient world and ultimately lead to his downfall. When Tukulti-Ninurta adorned the Assyrian throne, he inherited a formidable kingdom. But he was far too ambitious to disclaim the God of the *bicameral mind.* He boldly declared: “I am the Sun God of all people, King of all four quarters of the world”. He had a big ‘ego’ – a SUPEREGO. During the prime time of his reign, he had a stone altar made that was dramatically different from anything that preceded in the history of the world. On the carving of the altar’s face, Tukulti is shown twice; first he approaches the throne of the god, and then as he is kneeling before it – a double image. No god was present on the throne. That was an instance to show that the *bicameral mind* had *broken down.*

His first target were the Nairi tribes near Lake Van and he won them over with very little effort. He had a remarkable talent for incorporating conquered people into his expanding empire.

His defining achievement was the conquest of Babylon. His army breached Babylon's legendary defences in a swift campaign, and in an unprecedented move, he paraded the Kassite ruler through Ashur in chains. However, instead of destroying the Babylonian culture, Tukulti-Ninurta embraced it.

He built a new capital Kar-Tukulti-Ninurta which was a masterpiece of urban planning. But this ambitious project carried the seeds of his destruction. The construction costs strained the empire. There was no God speaker inside him, in the right hemisphere of his brain, to restrain his spending habits. In the long run, his own son, Ashur-nadin-apti, led the rebellion that ended in the King's assassination in his beloved capital city which was abandoned to desert winds. Yet his legacy endured – his methods of cultural integration. *(References 1-3)*

What God Wants Me For

Jesus, don't want me for sunbeam
Cause sunbeams are not made like me
And don't expect me to cry
For all the reasons you had to die
Don't ever ask your love of me.

Don't expect me to lie
Don't expect me to cry
Don't expect me to die for thee.

Oh, Jesus don't want me for a sunbeam
'Cause sunbeams are not made like me
And don't expect me to cry
For all the reasons you had to die
Don't ever ask your love of me.

Don't expect me to lie
Don't expect me to cry
Don't expect me to die for thee.

Oh, Jesus don't want me for a sunbeam
'Cause sunbeams are not made like me
And don't expect me to cry
For all the reasons you had to die
Don't ever ask your love of me. "

(Songwriters: Eugene Kelly/Frances McKee,
Domino Publishing Company, Evolution Media Ltd.,
Universal Music Publishing Group)

God is calling you to be a *light*, a beacon for His purpose in the world where there is *darkness*. But you are not guided by a *bicameral mind* any longer. There has been a breakdown of the *bicameral mind.* You have your own *consciousness* which is represented by your *ego*, which is your new guiding force. So, you are unable to follow.

Gods Reigned Supreme in Mesopotamia

Throughout Mesopotamia, in the early days, all lands were owned by god and the Kings of different city-states were 'tenant farmers' of the god. The god was not living; it was only a statue. He had his own 'great house' at the centre of a complex of temple buildings. The statue of the god was probably made of wood to be light enough to be carried about on the shoulders of priests. The larger god-houses had lesser courts surrounded by rooms for the use of the steward-kings and subsidiary priests.

In most Mesopotamian cities, the house of a chief god was the *Ziggurat*, a great rectangular tower, rising by diminishing stages to a shining summit on which there was a chapel.

Since the divine statue was the owner of the land and people were his tenants, the first duty of the steward-king was to serve the god in formal ritualistic as well as personal non-ritualistic ways like eating, drinking, music and dancing. They had to be washed and dressed, appeased with resting and sleeping, enjoying sex with other god-statues from time to time. They had to be provided with pleasant fragrance and aroma and taken out for drives – all most ceremoniously. Food for the god was placed on the table in front of him. He was left to enjoy his meal alone. After a suitable period of time, the steward-king entered the shrine room from a side entrance and ate what the god had left. The human beings heard the statues speaking to them regarding decisions about various aspects of agriculture.

However, it was not the ordinary citizens who heard the voices of the great gods who owned the cities. The ordinary citizen appealed to them only in some great crisis, and that too, only through intermediaries who were the personal gods. Their voices could be heard and obeyed. In every citizen's house, there was a room for the personal god.

Theocracy in Egypt

The protected homogeneity of Egypt allowed the perpetuation of a more archaic form of theocracy – the god-king. Egypt has an ancient religious creation narrative, centred in the city of Memphis (which is close to Cairo), and the god Ptah. According to this, the world was created through the power of Ptah's thought and divine speech. Ptah conceives of the whole existence in his mind and speaks it out. He gives form to all things. The other various gods are variations of Ptah's voice or 'tongue'. What Ptah is really commanding is indeed the *bicameral voices* which began, controlled and directed Egyptian civilisation.

Osiris was the primeval god-king of Egypt. In ancient Egyptian mythology, the first person known to have heard Osiris's voice was a man named Pamyles, a nobleman. According to Plutarch's account in Moralia, Pamyles heard an oracular voice at Thebes and was instructed to find and educate Osiris, who later became the ruler of Egypt and taught humanity agriculture and civilisation. While we understand that this was the first time that an oracular voice mentioned about Osiris, his voice, will and wisdom were sought by the deceased during their judgment. His voice-based guidance was a vital part of the sacred Mysteries of Osiris, which commemorated his death and rebirth.

Osiris was killed by his brother Set who wanted Osiris's throne. His sister-wife Isis found the body of Osiris and had kept it hidden in the reeds where it was found in dismembered form. Isis retrieved and joined the fragmented parts, then briefly revived him by use of magic. This spell gave her time to become pregnant by Osiris. Isis gave birth to Horus. Since Horus was born after Osiris's resurrection, he became thought of a representation of new beginnings and the vanquisher of usurped Set.

Ptah-Seker (who resulted from the identification of the creator god Ptah with the god of the dead Seker) thus gradually became identified with Osiris, the two becoming Ptah-Seker-Osiris. As the sun was thought to spend the night in the underworld, and was subsequently 'reborn' every morning, Ptah-Seker-Osiris was identified as the King of the underworld, god of afterlife, life, death, and regeneration.

Some scholars suggest that Osiris originated as a shepherd in the herding tribes of the Upper Nile. Recent researchers emphasize on the androgynous character of Osiris.

References

1. "Ancient Mesopotamia: 'The Land between Two Rivers", Spurlock Museum.
2. Leslie, "The Rise and Fall of Tukulti-Ninurta I: The King Who Built an Empire and Lost Everything", *Medium*, 17th January 2025.
3. Julian Jaynes, *The Origin of Consciousness in the Breakdown of the Bicameral Mind,* Boston, New York: A Mariner Book, Houghton Mifflin Company, 2000.

CHAPTER 14

Finding God in Your Body or in Something that You Love

Is There a God in the Gut

Steven Paul Jobs (Steve Jobs) came to the world in 1955 and left in 2011 at the young age of 56. There is no denial that he was one of the most outstanding technical wizards that the modern digital era has witnessed. A born change-seeker and change-maker, most interestingly, he combined with his technical acumen, an avid interest in spirituality, arts, and psychedelic experience.

Jobs had his spiritual journeys also. He was perhaps seeking the eternal truth: what is the purpose of this mortal life? He had visited the ashram of the North Indian Hindu saint Neem Karoli Baba. 'Autobiography of a Yogi' by Swami Yogananda was one of Jobs' most favourite reads. A copy of this book, contained in a beautiful basket was presented to everyone who attended his memorial service, pre-planned by him. A good part of his life, Jobs had looked inside in his pursuit for *self-realisation*. Nevertheless, in doing so, he had neglected a most vital part of his body which did not receive his attention while he was in good health.

In his deathbed speech, there was one para which was exposed to the general public by his sister four long years after his death. It said: "When a person goes into the operating room, he will realise that there is one book that he had not cared to read – *The Book of Healthy Life*."

Jobs had died of a gut-based cancer, a pancreatic neuroendocrinal tumour. There are no symptoms of this type of cancer in the early stage. The reason is simple: the friendly microbes (I call them 'F') go on fighting the pathogenic bacteria, but when they start losing, symptoms start showing up – lack of appetite and weight loss. When Jobs realised that he had neglected to pay attention to his gut health, he had heard his parting *gut whispers*: "You are a loser......you are a loser. You lost in the battle as you couldn't realise the truth......what was equally important. You had looked only on the outside." He had immediately uttered on this self-realisation: "Oh, Wow! Oh, Wow!! Oh, Wow!".

Is There a God in the Piano

Thomas 'Blind Tom' Wiggins (1849-1908) was an American pianist and composer. He had numerous compositions published and had a lengthy and largely successful performing career throughout the US. During the 19th century, Wiggins was one of the best-known BLACK musicians (After getting to know about the pie of the COSMOS, I get fascinated with Dark Matter and Dark Energy).

Blind at birth, Tom was sold in 1850 along with his enslaved parents to the Georgia lawyer General James Neil Bethune.

Because Tom was blind, he could not perform work normally demanded of slaves. Instead, he was left to play and explore in his Master's huge estate. Tom developed an interest in the piano after hearing the instrument played by Bethune's daughters.

By age 4, he gained access to the piano and by age 5, he had composed his first tune, The Rainstorm, after a torrential downpour on a tin roof.

Neighbour Otto Spahr observed: "Tom seemed to have only two motives in life: the gratification of his appetite (for survival) and his passion for music. He made the piano go for 12 hours out of 24."

In 1860, he performed at the White House in front of the President of USA.

The legendary Sir Elton John had composed a special song in honour of Blind Tom.

Is There a God in Jazz

Thanks to my good friend Dipankar Gangopadhyay who just reminded me to explore the King of Jazz Herbie Hancock (1940-born) to get convinced how spiritual faith makes a top musician.

Herbie Hancock the winner of 1 Academy Award, 14 Grammy Awards and the 2025 Polar Music Awardee – repeatedly acknowledges and celebrates God's sovereignty and providential control of history. In both personal letters and public presentations, he affirms his belief that God controls all events.

Herbie started playing the piano at the age of 7 and got recognised as a child prodigy. The King of Jazz, never had a jazz teacher. He developed his ear and a sense of harmony which forms the heart of jazz music, by listening to the records of great jazz pianists.

Hancock has practiced Nichiren Buddhism since 1972. He recites a Buddhist chant every day. He has also authored a book 'Reaching Beyond: Improvisation on Jazz, Buddhism, and a Joyful Life' (2017). Listen to his lecture on 'Buddhism and Creativity' at Harvard University where he holds a Visiting Professor's post.

The lecture was delivered at the 'Mahindra Humanities Centre' at the Harvard University. This centre has been funded by the Indian Mahindra and Mahindra Group. Anand Mahindra is an alumnus of both Harvard College and Harvard Business School.

God Saved Him

Cat Stevens is a British top pop singer whose records and CDs have sold in millions. He has an extraordinary golden voice as if it comes from the AKASHA above.

In 1968, the heavy workload of touring, media and commitments and the perks of a popstar lifestyle, took its toll and Cat Stevens contracted a potentially fatal bout of TB which hospitalised him for several months. It was during this LEAN time, that he began a significant process of self-reflection and search for the purpose of life.

In 1975, Cat experienced another momentous life-changing event. While swimming in the Pacific Ocean, he began losing his self-control and was almost getting drowned. He immediately called to GOD pleading that should he be saved, he would dedicate his life to God's service. GOD listened to him and a gentle wave delivered him to the shore and safety. His brother gave him a copy of the Islamic sacred text Quran which he read with great interest and found out what he was looking for. He got converted from Christianity to Islam and became known as Yusuf Islam in 1978. He then amazed the world by WALKING AWAY from FAME and WEALTH to lead a modest family life and dedicate himself to charitable work.

God in His Shenai

'Even if the world ends, music will still survive. Music has no caste.'

—*Bharat Ratna Late Ustad Bismillah Khan*

Ustad Bismillah Khan had played in his shenai a song which carried the massage as below:

> 'Oh, God! You shower so much happiness, but we are so far from you – we suffer from illusion to find happiness from elsewhere where something is missing. Our soul longs to go to you as you are our real home where it could finally find solace and peace'.

When the great artist based at Varanasi was asked to the stay back in America and the offer was fabulous for teaching music there, he said can you give me Ganges and the temple of Balaji where every morning I practice to worship the Hindu God. He instantaneously declined the offer as he was a rare highly spiritual musician who never played to accumulate wealth and fame like most musicians do. Music was God for him.

He had said in one interview: "One night, I was playing deep in meditation ('Savikalpa Samadhi' – 'Flow Brain State'), I smelled some indescribable scent – a mixture of sandalwood and jasmine. When I opened my eyes, there was Lord Balaji himself standing in front of me, exactly as he is pictured. The God said – 'Play my son – play for the mankind' – but I couldn't believe my eyes and was sweating profusely in wonder and excitement. I stopped playing and the Lord disappeared.'

A man who will feel the presence of God nearby, for him wealth and fame were like pebbles in front of the real pearls that he got by his devotion to God.

Born a Muslim, he was devoted to the Hindu God Balaji and had adopted a brilliant musical genius – a girl from a Hindu high caste Brahmin family – Dr Soma Ghosh (nee Chakraborty), PhD in Music from the Benares Hindu University.

God was His Companion

Ustad (Baba) Allauddin Khan (1862–1972), the most versatile instrumentalist and noted music composer and teacher had fled from home and came to Calcutta where he had his first vocal music lessons.

Maihar was the place where he had finally settled down as the court musician of the Maharaja of Maihar. When he first arrived at Maihar, penniless, a local resident Suraj Sahai gave him shelter in his house. Every day, Suraj used to visit the Sharda temple which was on top of a hill. Alauddin used to accompany him by climbing up and down 552 steps. While Suraj Babu would be busy inside the temple offering puja, Allauddin used to sit outside and play the shenai. The Goddess must have been charmed at his shenai badan and showered blessings on him. It didn't take long for Allauddin to get the job as Maihar Raja's court musician.

In Maihar he used to play multiple instruments – wind, strings and percussion, started a musical band with orphaned children and developed a few new Ragas.

Music was God for him and, like Ustad Bismillah Khan, Allauddin also firmly believed that music had no religion, caste or creed. He laid the foundation of the famous Maihar gharana to which many top musicians belonged.

Khan Sahib was a devoted Muslim but, at the same time, he used to worship Hindu Gods and Goddesses, especially Sharda – who is Goddess Saraswati. He got his daughter Annapurna, a Muslim girl, married to a high caste Hindu boy, Ravi Shankar Chowdhury who later became Pt. Ravi Shankar.

God Resided in His Single Lung

The inimitable Hindustani classical vocalist Pandit Kumar Gandharva's family home in Diwas, Madhya Pradesh was near a temple for a local goddess. One day, around noon time, Pandit Ji heard a goat being dragged to be sacrificed to the goddess. The relentless noon sun, the goat's bleating, and his imagination of absolute FEAR that the poor helpless animal was feeling inspired him to write a composition and the outcome was:'Bachale Mori Maan'.

Conventionally, the themes in Hindustani composition have been mostly romantic (shringara), devotional (bhakti) or valorous (veera). So bringing 'fear' (bhaya) as a 'rasa' or 'emotion' and the bleating of the goat as a sound in the ambit of Hindustani music is a clear evidence of his risk-taking courage and uniqueness. Gandharva could identify himself with the poor animal, but being only a human and not God, could only sing a song for it to develop awareness against animal sacrifices as he could not rescue him from the hands of the butchers.

Pt. Gandharva, during the prime of his youth had been confined to bed for years being afflicted by a bad type of tuberculosis which had damaged one of his lungs. It was during that prolonged illness, that he had his first spiritual awakening.

Kanada writer U R Ananthamurthy wrote about an interaction with Kumar Ji:

> "Half-asleep eyes, high-pitched voice, breathing through just one lung, balding head, I was astonished that God became a tenant and prospered in a place like that."

CHAPTER 15

Godly Gems

Rage

I will not utter your name again
I will not work as you ask any more.
The more words I use, the more absorb it becomes.
I speak of your attributes and find flaws of my own speech.

Who is going to make all those trips to your house and back
Any more? Certainly not me!
Says Tuka, haven't I got all that I want
Right here with me?

[Poem by Tukaram (1608–1650), Hindu Saint from Maharashtra who just disappeared in the forty-eighth year of his life. He had denounced mechanical rites, rituals, sacrifices, vows and instead encouraged direct form of bhakti (devotion). All mechanistic religious rites and rituals are related to the left hemisphere of the brain whereas seamless devotion is a right hemisphere trait. Tukaram encouraged kirtan as a music imbued, community-oriented group singing and dancing form of bhakti.

His most devout followers believed that Lord Vishnu (Vitthal) himself carried Tukaram away.

This poem has been translated by Dilip Chitre and included in Eating God: A Book of Bhakti Poetry, edited by Arundhati Subramaniam and published by Penguin, UK.]

Regret and Gratitude

I was so far from You
Yet to me You were always so close
I wandered lost in the dark
I closed my eyes to all the signs You put in my way
I walked every day
Further and further away from You
Allah You brought me home
I thank You for every breath I take
Alhamdu lillah, Alhamdu lillah
All praise is to Allah, All praise is to Allah
Alhamdu lillah, Alhamdu lillah
All praise is to Allah, All praise is to Allah
I never thought about
All the things that You have given to me
I never thanked You once
I was too proud to see the truth
And prostrate to You, until I took the first step
I was too proud to see the truth
And prostrate to You, until I took the first step
And that's when You opened the doors for me
And now, Allah, I realise what I was missing
By being far from You
Alhamdu lillah, Alhamdu lillah
Alhamdu lillah, Alhamdu lillah
All praise is to Allah, All praise is to Allah
Alhamdu lillah, Alhamdu lillah
Alhamdu lillah, Alhamdu lillah
All praise to Allah, All praise is to Allah
Allah, I want to thank You
I want to thank You for all the things
You've done for me through all my
years I've been lost

I wanna thank You for all the things that You've done
You've done for me through all my years I've been lost
You guided me from all the ways that were wrong
Indeed, You gave me hope. O Allah, I wanna thank You
I wanna thank You for all the things You've done
You've done for me through all my years I've been lost
You've guided me from all the ways that were wrong
I wanna thank You for bringing me home
You've guided me from all the ways that were wrong
I wanna thank You for bringing me home
Alhamdu lillah, Alhamdu lillah
All praise is to Allah, All praise is to Allah
Alhamdu lillah, Alhamdu lillah
All praise is to Allah, All praise is to Allah
Alhamdu lillah, Alhamdu lillah
Alhamdu lillah, Alhamdu lillah!!

[Lyric & Composition: Maher Zain who is a 1981-born Lebanese-Swedish Islamic singer, songwriter, and music producer. This song is taken from his debut album Thank You Allah – an internationally most successful album produced by Awakening Records in 2009. The song expresses the singer's regret for keeping himself autistic towards Allah; now he has realised that he had been at fault all these years – but most benevolent Allah had never been unkind and away from him. Throughout the song, he is expressing his soul-felt gratitude.]

Don't you feel lucky for what all have you got from God over all these years?

God is What You have in Your Mind

Seeing is one thing looking is another.

If both come together, that is god.
If you look for an elephant he comes as an elephant.
If you look for a tree he is a tree.
If you look for a mountain he'll be a mountain.

God is what you have in your mind.
If you look for an empty space
he appears as space.
If you look for an ocean he'll be an ocean.
If you look for a city he will come as a city.

God is what you have in your mind

If you think of the god on the hill married to the goddess that's who you'll see.

What you look for is the god in you.
What you see is the god out there.

God is what you have in your mind!

This poem was composed by Tallapaka Annamacharya (1408–1503), also popularly known as Annamayya. He was a Telugu musician, composer, and Hindu saint. He is the earliest known Indian musician to compose songs called *samkirtanas*, which were in the praise of Venkateswara, a form of Vishnu. The essence of this poem is God is what we think him to be. But your real goal ought to be to look for God in you. The Telugu poem has been translated into English by John Stratton Hawley and Mark Juergensmeyer. *(Reference 1)*

Reference

1. Ed. Arundhathi Subramaniam, *A Book of Bhakti Poetry: Eating God*, Gurugram, UP, India; Penguin Random House India, 2014.

CHAPTER 16

True Religion

"We are ungrateful to our 'existence'. It has given so much to us, and without our asking. And, we are such ungrateful creatures, that we don't even bother to look around what 'existence' is continuously doing for us, the sun, the moon, the stars, the trees, the birds, the animals, the people. You are living in a tremendously beautiful dream; but you have to be awake about it. Then only a gratefulness arises – I call that gratefulness, 'true religion'."

—OSHO
The Swan Song

You Start Dying Slowly

You start dying slowly
if you do not travel
if you do not read,
If you do not listen to the sounds of life
If you do not appreciate yourself
You start dying slowly.

When you kill your self-esteem,
When you do not let others help you,
You start dying slowly;

If you become a slave of your own habits;
Walking everyday on the same paths;
If you do not change your own routine
If you do not wear different colours

Or you do not speak to those you don't know
You start dying slowly.

If you avoid to feel passion
And their turbulent emotions;
Those which make your eyes glisten
And your heart beat fast
You start dying slowly.

If you do not risk what is safe for the uncertain,
If you do not go after a dream,
If you do not allow yourself
At least once in your lifetime,
To run away........
You start dying slowly!!!

(Pablo Neruda, Spanish Poet, 1971 Literature Nobel Laureate)

If you do not think of God
And speak to Him daily
You start dying slowly!!
(Don't Be Autistic Towards God!)

(The bold lines are my addition to Neruda's beautiful poem)